SOLDIER ON

Published by Endeavor Literary Press
P.O. Box 49272
Colorado Springs, Colorado 80949
www.endeavorliterary.com

ISBN Print Version: 978-1-7368734-4-1
ISBN Ebook: 978-1-7368734-5-8

Cover Design: James Clarke (jclarke.net), United Kingdom
Editor: Glenn McMahan

CONTENTS

SOLDIER ON

By Bracha Horovitz

with Sophie Paulson

ENDEAVOR
LITERARY PRESS

For my parents, Chaim and Chana,
who were the inspiration and guiding force throughout my life.

For my late husband, Zvi,
whose creativity and unflinching determination
provided a firm foundation for our family.

And for Ronny,
who gave me the life-altering opportunity to peel back the layers of superficiality
in the world and to see instead the true beauty and richness of life.

CHAPTER ONE

THE BACKPACK

The night obscured the desert around us. For hours, all I had seen was the rhythmic bobbing of the helmet and rucksack in front of me, a sight accompanied by the sound of our boots marching through the rocky valley. The straps of my backpack gouged painfully into my shoulders.

My companions and I had undergone three months of rigorous military training. This march, a culminating and grueling eight-hour ordeal, would earn us our berets and secure our status as Israeli soldiers.

We had begun our trek on the previous evening, before the searing orange sun had set beyond the distant plateaus. At that moment, we had felt strong, competent, and curiously relaxed. We had faith in our training and in each other.

It was 1970. I was an eighteen-year-old Israeli girl propelled into adulthood by my compliance with Israel's Security Service Law. This law mandated that, upon turning eighteen, all Israeli citizens (with few exceptions) had to serve in the Israel Defense Forces, or IDF. I had agreed willingly, even eagerly, but with little grasp of what my compliance would entail.

Alongside the eleven other women in my squadron, I had learned survival skills, weapons training, physical endurance, and military discipline. I had jumped out of planes, navigated through uncharted terrain using only a compass, taken thirty-second showers, and, unbelievably, looked in the mirror one day to see an IDF soldier looking back at me. I had been transformed from a girl into a woman. By completing this *masa kumpta* (beret march), I hoped to impress my superiors and hear them say, "She's ready."

That was at the start of the hike. Now I found myself faltering. We had been marching in darkness for hours, and I still had no way of knowing how much farther we had to go. My pack seemed heavier with every step. I wondered whether the others were struggling as much as me. Doubts about my competency darkened my morale like the night that enveloped me.

Who am I kidding? I wondered. *I don't belong here. I'm not ready!*

The march was calling my bluff. My mind and body had never felt so battered. The muscles in my shoulders burned and I could feel blisters forming on my feet, but I was most worried about losing the mental battle. I tried to remember something from training that would help me press on, some helpful practice or inspiring phrase. But all I could hear was my ragged breathing. I wondered if my instructors and team had seen my weakness all along.

Abruptly, the terrain became steep. I still could not see much, but I suspected that we would next ascend the switchbacks that led to the top of the limestone bluffs looming over us. The Negev, a desert in southern Israel where we had been marching, is not flat. It is full of jagged cliffs, arid valleys, and dunes dotted by low brush and chalky boulders. Our destination, we soon discovered, was Masada, an ancient first-century fortress on top of a plateau. Our military leaders certainly chose this destination to inspire us, for at Masada, in about 73 CE, fewer than a thousand Jews had taken a bold stand against a Roman legion. If the first portion of the hike had depleted us, the arduous climb to Masada was about to bleed us dry.

This is it, I thought. *I will be revealed as my squadron's weakest link. I can't give any more.*

Suddenly, the woman who had been marching in front of me for hours disappeared from my sight. I tripped on the fallen soldier and landed on the ground. The fall gave me some relief, for I could rest on my side. The ground supported my pack's weight, alleviating my shoulders. But I knew I couldn't stay there for long. Forcing myself into a sitting position, I inspected the woman who had collapsed in front of me. She was sprawled on the gravel with a look of defeat on her dusty face. I could tell that she, too, wanted to quit. Her eyes expressed my own desperation, and that, mysteriously, unlocked a hidden reserve of strength. Moving to a crouched position in front of the woman, I stood up, removed her pack, and strapped it to my chest. Another soldier helped our fallen friend get up, dusted her off, and shoved a water canteen into her hands. We nodded to each other and resumed the march.

As I fell back into formation, I wondered if I had been foolish in choosing to carry another pack. But I soon realized that I could carry the additional weight. In fact, I felt buoyed, perhaps because I was helping a friend in need. Just when I thought I had reached the ceiling of what my body could handle, I discovered that the ceiling was higher than it had seemed. I recognized again that my most formidable enemy was my mind. Doubt, exhaustion, insecurity, frustration, and shame had convinced me, falsely, that I had been operating at full capacity. I had limits, of course, but the second backpack served as a reminder that many limits are imaginary. As we climbed, I knew that I was learning something important. By helping another person in need, I could do more than I thought possible. It was a lesson I did not want to forget.

As I trudged on in the dark, I heard someone start to sing behind me. The song reminded me of home, Ein Kerem, of walking confidently through the cobblestone square hand-in-hand with my father, the man I most loved and respected in the world. In many ways, I was marching that night because of him. His adolescence had been darkened by World War II. Despite everything he had lost, he had emerged into manhood with a determination to not allow evil to win. That resolve led him to raise his young family in what was then the newly established state of Israel. The choice was, for him, an opportunity to ensure the dignity, safety, and legacy of the Jewish people. His strength and devotion to Israel seemed to ignite in others a similar fervor. It certainly had that effect on me. I wanted to make my father, and the nation he championed, proud.

The singing began to swell through the ranks like the Negev's floodwaters in spring. I joined in, surprised by my own exuberance. Moments earlier, I had thought my lungs would collapse, but the song revitalized me, reawakening my kinship with the women who marched alongside me. When we had first arrived at basic training, we had been complete strangers. Now, after three months of learning, training, and testing, we had forged an intense bond. We had made each other laugh, seen each other cry, and experienced the limits of what our minds and bodies could withstand. This march would not break us.

Our songs and shouts of encouragement had carried us a great distance that night. Soon, we could make out the faint outline of the Dead Sea in the distance. At the next switchback, I saw a warm glow behind the Moab Mountains. As we hiked up the steep plateau, I hoped to soon see an expansive view of Israel, a vision that would make the long, dismal night seem like a remote memory.

I heard a shout from above. News trickled down the slope. Sure enough, the looming walls of the fortress were not far away. The sky was steadily filling with color. Joyful relief was palpably flowing through the ranks.

My shoulders protested one more time, but, paradoxically, the pain filled me with gratitude. My pack was not a burden. It was a friend not a foe. By carrying its weight, I found resilience. It had equipped me to soldier on.

CHAPTER TWO

SABRA

"What's on your mind, *yaldati*?"

I heard that affectionate word, which literally means *my dear daughter,* when I was eight years old and walking in uncharacteristic silence beside my father. The sun had just dropped behind the distant Judean hills. A golden glow spread over the horizon and across the forests and vineyards below. For all its familiarity, this was the part of the day that I anticipated most, because I always spent it with my father.

Evening walks accentuated the regular rhythm of our relationship. Multiple times a week, my maternal grandmother would come over to spend the day at our house and eat dinner with our family. After dinner, my father would stand up from the table, kiss my mother on the cheek, and ceremoniously offer his arm to my grandmother.

"May I escort you home, madam?"

Savta, knowing her part, would smile and roll her eyes at her theatrical son-in-law before taking his arm. Then my father would turn to me.

"But wait!" he'd exclaim. "Who will escort *me* home?"

"Me, me, Abba! I will!"

His question was as predictable as my answer, but that didn't keep us from reenacting the scene with gusto every time.

That night, however, something was different. Despite having a full stomach, I felt emotionally drained. When my father asked who would escort him home, I hesitated. I looked at my father and could see the expectation on his face. I couldn't let him down, so I dutifully blurted out my line.

"Me, me, Abba! I will."

As we strolled the leisurely mile to my grandmother's home, I resolved to conceal my distress. My father and grandmother happily conversed while I remained silent. We said goodbye to my grandmother and began to walk back to our house.

My father knew me too well. We had barely turned the first corner when he placed his arm around my shoulder and asked what was on my mind. Staring down at my dusty sandals, I wondered what I could say. I was loath to hide anything from him, but I also felt apprehensive about asking him the question that I had been pondering.

"What is it?" he asked. He squatted down and looked me in the eye.

His gentleness made me yield. "It's nothing much. I've just been bothered by something all day."

He raised his eyebrows.

"Well, it's just that one of the girls at school told me she has four grandparents," I said. "But I only have one."

My father said nothing. He stood up and resumed his stride. For a moment, I thought he was not going to respond.

"My!" he said playfully. "Four grandparents? Your friend's cheeks must be very pink from all the pinching!"

He reached over to lovingly pinch me like Savta always did, but I dodged him. I knew he was trying to distract me, and I was determined to get an answer to my question.

"My friend said that she had never met her grandparents because they all live far away," I said while looking at my father out of the corner of my eye.

"Yes, not everyone's Savta lives so close," he said. "You should count yourself very lucky."

"Do *I* have grandparents far away?" I asked.

Savta had once told me that my grandfather (her husband) had died from tuberculosis when my mother was a young girl. My father, however, had never told me about *his* parents. Most children live with a certain amount of mystery and puzzlement surrounding their parents' origins. Until that day, I too had suffered from the same youthful myopia. It seemed to me that my father, who had boundless joy and energy, had simply sprung up from the dust of the ground.

"Ach, Bracha." His voice sounded far away. "Why do you ask this now? You do not want to know about such things."

"But I *do* want to know, Abba!" I implored. My father's abnormal seriousness concerned me, but I also feared that my question, if left unanswered, would stalk me through the night. Seeing my desperation, he sighed deeply and, with his hand on my shoulder, steered me down an empty side street.

"I prefer not to dwell in the past," he told me. "But I'll try to tell you what I can."

I nodded.

"So, you want to know what happened to your other grandparents, my parents, yes?"

His blue eyes were intense—his most memorable and captivating physical trait—but I had never seen them so sorrowful. Dusk was settling in. There would be no easy exodus from the dark tunnel I'd steered us into. The only way out was through.

"Alright," he said. "The truth is, *yaldati,* I can't tell you *exactly* what happened to your grandparents."

I frowned.

"Listen," he said with a wavering voice. He cleared his throat and continued. "I can't tell you because I don't know."

I stared uncomprehendingly.

"I am only sure of one thing," he said. "You will never get the chance to meet them."

I looked at my father in horror. This was not what I had expected to hear. In the short time since I had first wondered about his parents, I had hoped to meet them. My father erased that hope.

Mercifully, he proceeded to tell me a little about their lives—a line here, a curve there, some faint shading. It was not the full picture I craved, but seeing his underlying pain, I knew I could not press for too much. Even a rough sketch was costly for him.

My father said he had grown up in Poland. His father had run a small tailor shop while my grandmother had looked after the home and their five kids. My father and his siblings had been raised to keep many Jewish traditions, but they felt only loosely linked to those roots. Growing up in a small, coastal town on the edge of the Baltic Sea, they felt as much like Poles as Jews. Unfortunately, my father explained, he had been born in a time when neither identity had been favorable. There had been mounting anti-Semitism and increasing tensions between Poland and Germany, a conflict that had been brewing since the end of World War I. By the time he was a teenager, my father said, Germany was eager to start a fight.

"What do you know about the Shoah?" my father asked.

I told him that I had learned in school that *shoah*, the Hebrew word for "catastrophe," was the name given to the atrocities committed against Jews during World War II. At age eight, I didn't know many details.

"Good," he said brusquely. "Then I'm sure you know about the German camps. My family and I were sent to one called Auschwitz." He paused. "Your grandparents died there. I was the only one of my family to survive."

My eyes welled up with tears. Perhaps the emotion in my father's voice and countenance revealed the magnitude of what his cautious wording concealed. I could not keep the tears from trickling down my cheeks. I felt robbed.

We walked in silence for a few moments before coming to a sudden halt. Looking up, I noticed my father staring at a green wall of cacti that lined the dusty road. The cacti, tall enough to tower over my father, had sharp needles protruding from large cladodes. These cacti grew prolifically throughout Israel's wilderness. In the villages, they served as natural fences, offering privacy and security to the homes they encircled.

"Do you see these?" my father asked, pointing to one of the cacti's egg-shaped fruits. He slipped off his sandal and used it to knock the bright red fruit to the ground. Then, avoiding its thorns, he picked it up and gingerly held it out for me to examine.

"We call this cactus and its little fruits a *sabra,*" my father said. "That's also what we call people like you, *yaldati.*"

"Me?"

"Yes. You and those who are the first of their families to be born in Israel," he told me. "Do you want to know why?"

I stared at the sabra fruit and nodded.

"Because the sabra cactus is resilient," he said. "It grows in very hot, barren climates where there is little rain and where the soil is rocky and unforgiving. The sabra is an amazing organism because it thrives where most plants can't. Do you understand?"

For anyone who knew him, my father's didactic tone was as familiar as his jokes and sarcasm. He was an instructor at the local agricultural school, so he often interrupted our walks to give me a nature lesson. My father loved drawing attention to the complexity of Israel's ecosystem, and he seemed to have a limitless knowledge about soil, farming, irrigation, and agricultural economics. Agriculture was more than a job to him; it was the means by which he could meet Israel's practical needs and contribute to its economic vitality. In his enthusiasm, my father often forgot to tailor his lessons to an age-appropriate audience. But even when I failed to understand the information he shared, his passion made boredom impossible.

I knew that the cactus lesson that day was about more than agricultural economics, but it was hard to understand why we were talking about sabras when I still had so many questions about his parents—the grandparents I had never met.

My father pulled a pair of work gloves out of his back pocket, put them on, and started to carefully pick spines out of the prickly fruit.

"When I was a boy in Poland, Bracha, there was no state of Israel. A few Jews were here in Palestine, but most of us were scattered all over the world. Some in Poland, like me, some in Bulgaria like your mother and Savta, some in Africa or the Orient . . ."

"The diaspora Jews!" I interjected, proud to have remembered such a big word in front of my father. "That's what my teacher called the Jews who were spread out!"

"Yes, that is what we were called," he said with a grimace. "You might hear things about the diaspora Jews, but you must not believe everything. The native generation, those who have lived here all along, cannot understand what life was like for us."

I kept listening as my father's hands expertly rubbed the needles off the sabra.

"Native Israelis say that the diaspora Jews had a privileged life in Europe or America, and that we should have heeded the Zionist call to return to Palestine while we still had the chance." His voice became more intense. "They assume that we had a choice to come here, and that our lives were easy! 'The diaspora Jew was not used to toil,' they say. 'He was a merchant, a lawyer, unaccustomed to hard labor. His hands were soft. His lifestyle made him feeble and submissive, otherwise he never would have allowed himself to be led like a sheep into the Shoah!'"

Then my father's voice broke.

"But they weren't *there*," he whispered. "They didn't see our strength. They didn't see the way . . ."

He trailed off, as if suddenly remembering that he was not alone.

"I'm sorry, *yaldati*," he said, collecting himself. "I did not mean for you to see me this way. But I have heard these comments too many times from my Israeli brothers and sisters, and it sickens me. They've formed an image of the diaspora Jew that is all wrong. It is the same revolting image that led to the death of my family, and your grandparents."

He then reached over and set the sabra fruit, now free of needles, in my open hand. It was nearly dark. I worked the sabra around in my hands, rubbing its smooth spots and feeling its weight.

"Do you feel that?" he asked. "Those scars are where the spines were. It's not easy to get to the sabra's skin, and even when you do, it's tough. If I were to cut it open, you would see how thick it is. But its thick skin protects something inside—a fruit that is soft and delicate. You bite into it and it almost melts in your mouth. The flavor is surprising, too! You've eaten it. Is the sabra's flavor bitter?"

I shook my head vehemently. My mother had often brought the fruit, already de-spined and skinless, home from the market for my sister and me to eat. We loved the sweet, juicy pulp.

"This is why your generation is called the Sabra generation," my father told me. "Your goodness is kept safe by a tough exterior. You're prickly. Resilient. Some would say you have grown up in a harsh and unforgiving environment, but you were built for this. You have the strength to survive."

I looked down at the fruit in my hand. I had seen a sabra cactus nearly every day of my life, but I had never known all that it represented.

My father carried on. "For too long, our people have been told we were too weak and fragile to survive. Like seeds, we were trampled on and scattered to the winds. But no longer! Our land has been restored to us. We have given you, our children, a place to put down roots. You will show the world what Israelis are really like, that no matter how many times we're pushed down, we rise again."

"Are you a Sabra too, Abba?" I asked.

"No, *yaldati*. Although sometimes I feel that I am."

As we started to walk again, my father described himself as part of the Pioneer generation. I could tell he was skipping details, but he told me that after surviving Auschwitz, at age nineteen, he had been transported to a refugee camp in Italy. While alone in a morass of physically and psychologically broken people, he said he had overheard conversations about how some survivors had planned to start over in America. That idea, he said, did not set well with him. As a survivor, he told me, he had come to see life as a profound gift. He yearned to live for a noble purpose.

"Zionist missionaries came to the refugee camp. They taught us about Palestine and showed us that it was our true homeland. Jews were not weak, they reminded us, but they believed that the diaspora had diffused our strength. Like the ancient Israelites in exile, we needed to return and reconstruct our walls, build a nest for our wandering people, establish a fortress from which to fight."

My father did not share much with me in that moment, but I later learned—over numerous years, little by little—the reasons for his heartbreak that evening. He had known the frustration of wanting to fight while powerless and imprisoned. He had seen people's rights and humanity stripped away. He had learned what it was like to see the face of evil, to know his father and mother had been treated as worthless objects. He had even witnessed his beautiful sister senselessly shot in the back.

These tragic experiences had motivated my father to help create a new Jewish nation, one that showcased the strength and dignity of its people and ensured their rights and safety. He chose that direction even though many people had urged him to get on a ship bound for America, to pursue what they imagined would be an easier life, especially because he no longer had parents. But he refused to listen to these well-meaning people. He wanted to create a future that could prevent the evil and suffering he had witnessed.

"The war for independence has ended," Abba said. "But the larger fight still isn't over."

I looked up at my father, confused.

"Every day we Pioneers get up and fight. We fight by cultivating the land so that it can sustain life. We fight by getting married and establishing homes, by being fruitful and multiplying." He pointed to the sabra in my hand. "And that is what we hope to produce. A generation of Sabras who will carry on our legacy."

CHAPTER THREE

EIN KEREM

My father arrived in Palestine in 1946, just a few years before representatives of the Jewish community and the Zionist movement would declare Israel a sovereign nation. Like many of the Pioneers who migrated to the land in droves, he was youthful, fervent, and eager to make the dream of *Eretz Israel* (the Land of Israel) a reality. Pride and excitement permeated the air. People sensed that the long exile was ending.

Conflict and the fear of war was also in the air. Many Jews initially had been willing to divide the land with the Arabs, but the Arabs were determined to share nothing with the Jews. Unsurprisingly, this increased the Jews' commitment to defend their ancestral homeland at all costs.

Eager to do his part, my father soon joined the Haganah, one of the underground militias that had existed for decades under the British Mandate, a 1918 League of Nations arrangement that had assigned Britain to govern the territories of Palestine and Transjordan. The Haganah, along with two other underground militias, coalesced to form the Israel Defense Forces when Israel became a state in 1948. He had fought in the war of independence that year, but doctors later discovered that he had a heart condition that prevented him from being in more combat situations. He eventually moved out of military service.

Determined to contribute to the cause, he decided to learn as much as he could about the land. Israel, he knew, would need a strong agricultural foundation to feed its citizens and support the economy. Without crops or commodities, Israel would not be able to buy, sell, or trade with other countries. Such a limitation would make it difficult to garner legitimacy and respect from the international community, which would in turn jeopardize the young nation's existence. So, he set to work studying how to establish an agrarian infrastructure.

My father was soon recruited by Rachel Yanait Ben-Zvi, the wife of Israel's second president, to be part of a school she was founding. Her mission was to gather the greatest agricultural minds—farmers, innovators, and educators—so that they could disseminate their knowledge and promote agricultural settlements in Israel. "To build and rebuild," as they often put it. My father was honored to be among those chosen for the task. Like many others who immigrated to Israel from the diaspora, he felt an inexplicable intimacy with the land from the moment he set foot within its borders. Studying agriculture and then educating many farmers was to him a calling. He firmly believed that living in Israel—to be a true Israeli—came with responsibilities.

Ben-Zvi's school where my father taught was in the village of Ein Kerem. Abandoned by the Arabs during the war for independence, most of the village's inhabitants were Pioneers who had come, like my father, to work at the Ein Kerem Agricultural School. When they arrived, each was told to pick one of the many deserted houses. My father chose a very small, simple house not far from the village center. Built with Jerusalem stone—a pale, dolomitic limestone—it had high, arched windows and a balcony. There was no electricity and no indoor bathroom, but the views compensated for what the house lacked.

Ein Kerem is situated in the mountains four miles southwest of Jerusalem. The village has a pastoral, isolated atmosphere. It seems to have escaped the fast-paced flow of history, and because of its proximity to the holy city, people often see it as hallowed ground. Some say that Ein Kerem's spiritual aura stems from its rich biblical background. Once occupied by the Canaanites, the region was overtaken by the people of Israel before it was settled by the tribe of Judah and named Beit HaKerem, or "House of the Vineyard." Mentioned in the Hebrew scriptures by figures such as Jeremiah and Nehemiah, it is also referenced in the New Testament as the "town in the hill country of Judea" where Mary, the soon-to-be-mother of Jesus, visited her pregnant cousin Elisheva (Elizabeth) before the birth of their sons. Thus, it is home to a church commemorating the birthplace of John the Baptist and a spring, known as "Mary's Spring," where Mary is believed to have drawn water on her visit. The spring is inscribed with words from Isaiah 55, which says, "Lo, everyone who thirsts, come to the waters," and is still flowing today. In Hebrew, Ein Kerem means "spring of the vineyard." These words evoke images of rushing water and plump, juicy grapes. So beautiful is the village and its surrounding area that it is easy to imagine burrowing a few feet underground to find milk pooling in the dirt, or leaning against a tree to find honey dripping like sap down its trunk. As a child, I gave little attention to my village's ancient ties or sacred history, but I felt the hallowedness of the place I called home.

Ein Kerem sits on the slope of a Judean hill. Scattered throughout the village are spots which offer unencumbered views of the stunning natural landscape that surrounds it. One of these locations, happily, was the balcony of my childhood home. I would often escape to that quiet place to observe the stirring panorama in solitude. My eyes would roam over the hills that teemed with a remarkable variety of trees and plants, including pine, cypress, juniper, sage, lavender, mulberry, and eucalyptus—to name a few. The view often called to mind the Torah verses I had read in school. "[A] good land—a land with brooks, streams, and deep springs gushing out into the valleys and hills; a land with wheat and barley, vines and fig trees, pomegranates, olive oil and honey" (Deuteronomy 8:7-8).

Standing on that balcony, I was overwhelmed by the land's opulence. The terrain and foliage seemed to flow down from the horizon and into our little valley, trickling into the village's tree-lined streets and over its garden walls. As if in response to this cascading beauty, the bells of local churches and monasteries would boldly ring. The clear sound would echo up the cobbled streets and narrow alleyways, across the terraced slopes, and into the hills beyond. There was reciprocity between Ein Kerem and the nature it inhabited. Perhaps because it was so undeveloped, and therefore had so many rough edges, I could never be sure where the wilderness ended and its cultivation began.

Within a couple years of moving to Ein Kerem and starting his job at the agricultural school, my father met and married my mother. She was nineteen and had grown up in Sofia, Bulgaria. The persecution of the Jews in World War II had forced her to flee with her family to Israel. After she met and married my father, the two of them began the difficult yet rewarding task of making their little house into a home.

When I was born in 1952, I was the first person on either side of my family to begin my life as a native Israeli. It would be years before I would realize how much this meant to my parents, who had survived the attempted extermination of our people. At sixteen, my mother had been uprooted from her life in Bulgaria to live as a refugee in a foreign country. Each in their own way, my parents had experienced incalculable loss, and yet they had chosen to keep moving forward by making a new life in what was then an undeveloped country—all because they wanted a better future for their children. They believed, along with many others, that the Holocaust would not have happened if the Jews had possessed a unified nation with a strong military. This belief compelled them to settle in Israel, to forfeit what they thought would be an easier life elsewhere. They wanted to build a nation where their children could have what had not been possible in the diaspora: a national identity, stability, and protection.

There was joy to be found in putting down roots, but the soil—literally and metaphorically—was rocky. Even the simplest tasks required struggle and perseverance. There were daily trips to the local food stall because we didn't have a refrigerator to preserve perishables. Food was prepared with only the simplest utensils and no appliances. Without plumbing, water had to be drawn from Mary's Spring and hauled back to the house. We washed clothes by hand, did our dishes in buckets, and scrubbed the floors on our hands and knees. My mother rarely took a break because, as her mother often told her, "What you do today, you don't have to do tomorrow." However, no matter how much we did, there was always more to do the next day. This humbling reality meant that I was never bored.

Despite the hard work, my childhood was infused with joy. The more effort we put into a task, the more enjoyment we received from its outcome. Making the daily trip to the food stall was inconvenient, but the produce was fresh and packed with flavor, never bland or stale. Preparing meals was an all-day endeavor, but when we finally sat down to eat, the food and fellowship gladdened our spirits. The labor that went into every chore was physically demanding, but it meant that we fell asleep quickly and slept soundly until daybreak.

Joy was also evident in the hearts of our friends and neighbors. All around me, I saw people who had every reason to complain or be resentful; no one came to Israel without having lost something, and many had lost everything. Upon arrival, they had encountered new hardships that left little time to grieve. Ours was a fast-moving society, with everyone working zealously to establish the nation. For most, the bustle of daily life was a mercy: It kept their minds from revisiting past traumas. To *not* delight in the simple things would be disrespectful of those who had perished in the Holocaust. And so, they chose joy.

The residents of Ein Kerem comprised an intricate ethnic and cultural mosaic. Everyone was so new in the country that they had not yet assimilated. As I walked through my village, I encountered an array of diverse clothing styles, a cacophony of foreign languages, and the aromas of exotic spices and perfumes. Curious and energized, I loved to take in the sights and sounds. Every stone-paved street and narrow alleyway was worth exploring because I never knew what I would see or who I would meet.

My parents—as was common in that neighborly time—often made afternoon visits to the homes of friends. I loved to go along, walking hand-in-hand with my father past the ivy-covered walls and bright bougainvilleas that splashed the streets with color. As we walked, we would talk or sing, waving at everyone we knew. These afternoon calls gave us a chance to socialize and relieve the burdens and pressures that had built up during the day. In our community, it was standard practice to keep tea or coffee and a light dessert ready for whoever might stop in. It was common for people to stay and chat until dark. After coaxing as many desserts from the adults as possible, children typically ran outside to play. I, however, was happiest when allowed to stay and listen to the grown-ups talk. Sometimes they discussed work, sometimes the past, but always they spoke of Israel. I absorbed it all like a sponge. There was so much I wanted to know, and so many interesting people to meet and stories to ponder. Each person's perspective shaped my nascent view of the world.

Although I loved being with adults, I also reveled in the vibrant social interactions at school. My classroom was a dazzling microcosm of Ein Kerem's ethnic melting pot. I had classmates from Yemen, Greece, Austria, Tunisia, Poland, Morocco, Germany, Turkey, Russia, Yugoslavia, Armenia, Iraq, and beyond. Each day, I heard a mesmerizing array of accents and observed a magnificent spectrum of skin tones and eye colors. Our differences were dramatic and extreme, but because *everyone* was so different from each other, no one stood out. We were all just Israeli children caught up in the joys of learning and playing together.

Even better than spending time together at school was the thrill of playing at my friends' houses afterwards. Some of my friends' homes were small and austere, and others were spacious and aesthetically furnished. Some parents were posh and highly educated, and others were brash and street-smart. The parents of my friends perhaps owned a shop or maybe a bookstore, or they earned wages as teachers and engineers. Some mothers cooked food that overwhelmed my senses before I even took a bite. I met women whose decorative talents made their homes seem like palaces. At some houses, I was pursued by a babbling throng of children. With so many options, I struggled to know where to go.

My school friends also came to my house. When they did, they frequently commented on the rich smells that greeted them from blocks away. My mother had a gift for making simple dishes taste and smell like they had been made at a gourmet restaurant. Each day, she would go to the market and select a handful of ingredients, always making sure that they were the freshest, most flavorful ingredients she could buy. She then combined them in remarkable, artful ways. Her food blessed my friends, especially those whose parents worked outside the home and therefore did not cook much for them. Many of my friends were also amazed by our home. Although by no means large or ornate, it was bigger than the cramped Jerusalem apartments in which many of them lived, and it had a yard with expansive views. All the same, it was clear that we lived simply. My mother was often chopping vegetables or defeathering a chicken at one end of the kitchen table while we completed homework at the other end. Our play included singing, dressing our dolls, carousing outdoors, or inventing innocent mischief. Together with neighborhood children, we played hopscotch or hide and seek. We could often be found up a tree talking or somewhere picking wild pomegranates and figs—eating them until we were no longer hungry for supper.

Despite the plethora of kids, I often played alone. I found great satisfaction in walking by myself through my village or its surrounding countryside. Intimately connected to nature, I often wrote poems or sang songs about the land. I loved to climb trees, build forts, eat wild fruit, and pick vibrant bouquets of flowers, which I used to decorate my room. Making spaces beautiful brought me joy, and once my room was set in order and decorated with all of the treasures I had found on my walks, I would look for ways to spruce up the rest of the home, even if it meant cleaning or organizing while my mom was away. I loved watching her face light up when she arrived at home to find the floors shining or a beautiful arrangement of wildflowers sitting on the kitchen table.

CHAPTER FOUR

ABBA AND EEMA

My childhood was wrapped in love, cultural diversity, and natural beauty, but as I grew older, I awakened to the grief and loss that pervaded my community's soul. In Ein Kerem, nearly everyone the age of my parents or older had experienced the war and the Holocaust. As a result of the devastation, daily life had a quiet undercurrent of suffering. Some residents, like my mother, had been spared from physical harm and had emerged, mercifully, with their families intact, but no one had escaped unscathed. Everyone mourned the losses, either through death or separation, of dear friends and neighbors. The life they knew before the war had been destroyed. Others, like my father, had directly experienced the cruelty and dehumanization of the Nazi camps. In addition to enduring great physical suffering themselves, they had witnessed friends, loved ones, and strangers sent to death. Unspeakable evil had barged into their homes, killed the people they loved, and detonated their sense of dignity. To be hopeful seemed foolish. Already living in diaspora, the Jews had been displaced even from their displacement, forced to scrape together what they could from the rubble and build a new life.

Instead of succumbing to despair, my parents' generation had picked themselves up from the dust, set their eyes on the horizon, and kept moving forward. In Israel, a collective voice seemed to say, "You may have knocked us down, but we won't stay down, and we certainly won't let it happen again." I learned as a child that to be Israeli was to be resilient.

In poetry and literature, *resilience* means to recover after hardship. The storm comes and the reed bends, but after the winds subside, the reed returns to its upright vitality. My parents embodied this resilience in different ways. My mother poured her attention and energy into providing my sister and me with a safe and wholesome home environment. She struggled with self-pity and a victim mentality, but she battled against these feelings by always staying busy. She worked from dawn to dusk to make sure that the house was neat, that our clothes were clean, and that meals were prepared with excellence. Like my father, she did not speak much about her past; she only shared vignettes from time to time.

She had grown up in Sofia, Bulgaria with her mother, brother, and sister. Her father had died of tuberculosis when she was only three. Among her earliest memories was the trauma of watching him fall ill and die alone in quarantine. She did not share much else about her childhood, at least with me, but she expressed love for Sofia and the life she had there. Sadly, when she was sixteen, she had to leave her home behind. Early in World War II, Hitler had demanded that all Jews in Bulgaria be deported. Boris III, then king of Bulgaria, had resisted Hitler's demands by stalling. That gave thousands of Jews time to evacuate. My mother had a few vivid memories of the day she left home. She remembered the feeling she had as she latched the suitcase that held her only possessions, and she remembered her grief while standing in the front garden, looking back at her house, knowing that she would probably never return. She could recall the surreal walk to the schoolyard where, instead of lingering outside with her friends before class, she and her family would congregate with other Jews as they awaited the trucks that would transport them out of Hitler's reach.

My mother's family fled from danger without knowing exactly where they would land. It must have been a journey fraught with danger and delay, because by the time they finally arrived in Ein Kerem, my mother was nineteen. Her siblings did not stay there long; instead, they moved to other places in Israel while my mother and grandmother stayed in Ein Kerem.

Soon after her arrival, my mother met my father while walking with a friend to the village's spring. Knowing my father's magnetism, I can only imagine how striking he must have seemed. He was twenty-four, with sandy brown hair, a ruddy complexion, and clear blue eyes that probably made her melt. Then there was his dynamic personality: charming and lighthearted without being flippant, wise and earnest without being somber. I have no doubt that my mother was drawn to him from the moment they met, even before she learned about his tragic past, his work in the Haganah, or his contribution to the community as an instructor at the agricultural school.

My father's vitality somehow transcended the hardships of his life. Growing up in a tiny Polish town and in a large Jewish family with four siblings, he likely did not lack companionship. He adored his two sisters, Leah and Rachel, and treasured a salvaged photo of them for the entirety of his life. When war descended on Europe, he and his family were carted off like cattle to Auschwitz in the south of Poland. I do not know how he recovered his soul from that experience, but he did.

My father did not typically talk about those experiences. It was as if his grief was held in by a towering dam, and the floodgates usually had only two settings: all the way shut or all the way open; nothing in between. He saw, I presume, no way to regulate a safe flow of emotion. Rather than opening the floodgates and potentially drowning others in his sorrow, he usually kept the dark waters safely contained.

However, on rare occasions he would allow a few haunting memories to leak out, as he had done on the night I had asked about my grandparents. When I was older, for example, he told me about his arrival at Auschwitz. Standing in a procession of men, women, and children, he remembered shuffling miserably toward an SS officer at the front of the line. With a cursory glance at each person, the officer would bark out an order and wave them in one direction or the other. Left or right. Death or labor. The old, the weak, and the trembling were deemed worthless and sent for extermination. The young, the broad-shouldered, the ones with defiance in their eyes, were deposited in labor camps where many would experience a slower, but just as demoralizing, death.

I could imagine the churning in my father's stomach as he watched each person receive a sentence. Where was his family? Which direction had they been sent? What would the SS officer see when his turn came?

"When he got to me," my father told me, "the officer looked me up and down, met my eyes for just a moment, and clapped me forcefully on the back. I was bound for the labor camp. I'll always remember that. He clapped me on the back."

For a long time, I could not make sense of the pride in my father's voice when he told me that story. What that Nazi officer had done was despicable. With each callous wave of his hand, he had destroyed lives and families. The thought of that hand on my father's shoulder made me shudder. Over time, however, I came to realize that the officer's impersonal gesture had affirmed something in my father that had, undoubtedly, sustained his hope while in the labor camp. The clap on his back had communicated to my father that the German officer had seen his strength. In an odd way, this affirmed my father's humanity. Even though it was offered by a merciless man, I think it later helped my father rebuild his life.

My father had grown up in a time of rising anti-Semitism. Propaganda portraying Jews as subhuman and disposable had become mainstream. Hate crimes against them took place regularly. Evil and fictitious stereotypes had seeped into the German mindset, and into the views of other groups. For decades, Zionist Jews had vehemently exhorted their scattered brethren to return to Palestine. Unfortunately, one way they did this was to feed the vitriol by creating a grotesque, false representation of the diaspora Jew. In broad, imprecise strokes, it painted them as spineless and weak. According to this stereotype, they had chosen professions that had made them pale-skinned, soft-handed, and accustomed to affluence. Meanwhile, the Zionists claimed, the diaspora Jews ceded more and more of their dignity and rights. They presumed that wealth, comfort, and lethargy had sedated the diaspora Jews into subservience. Sadly, this image was propagated throughout Jewish communities by some groups of Jews. In the eyes of the Zionists, the only way for Jews to prove their strength was to be in Palestine. Everyone else was weak by default. This falsehood was often absurdly cited as the reason for the Jews' suffering during the Holocaust. This ridiculous generalization had a sickening impact on millions of people. Even after the Holocaust, diaspora Jews who immigrated to Palestine were often met with quiet suspicion or direct contempt by Hebrew "natives" and Zionists. With history on our side, this malicious lie is now exposed for the venom it was.

My father never admitted it openly, but the pride I heard in his voice when he told his story about the German officer suggested that he had struggled with that negative stereotype. Therefore, it was important for others to understand that he had not been spineless, and that being in diaspora did not automatically make a person weak or passive.

How anyone could think that my father was weak is beyond me. He had survived a Nazi concentration camp and had progressed in life despite the loss of his family! To the best of my knowledge, he did not know what had happened to his family while he was there—except for one sister. One day he caught sight of her as she walked across a wide courtyard. Then he heard the sound of a gunshot echo off the walls. He watched as his beloved sister fell to the ground, mid-stride. The Nazis, in a nihilistic act, had shot her in the back. It seemed they had used her for target practice.

When he told me about this pointless horror, I wanted to scream at the injustice. I could not understand what would compel someone to do something so heartless and unprovoked. How could anyone be so depraved? I abhorred the thought that my father had suffered such tragedy alone and that other, more horrific memories might live inside his mind.

My father left Auschwitz not knowing whether his parents and remaining siblings were dead or alive. In the Italian refugee camp and for many years after, he listened as much as possible to a radio station whose sole mission was to help people reconnect with missing relatives and friends. Through these broadcasts, my father did find a second cousin, and (perhaps through other means) he found an older brother. Sadly, he never heard anything about his parents and other siblings. Although he did not know it at the time, when Auschwitz was shut down and its inhabitants were liberated by the Soviet army in 1945, my father was orphaned and alone. Not yet in his twenties and still grappling with trauma and grief, he was forced to face serious questions about his future. Where would he go? How would he use his freedom?

In Italy, he met Zionist missionaries who began telling him about the homeland and their grassroots movement, underway since the late 1800s, that had been working toward the establishment of a Jewish state in Palestine. There had already been decades of conflict, and more would come, but the missionaries were full of hope. Now that the world was starting to see the horrible persecution of the Jews, they believed that other nations would be moved to action. They believed that the success of the Zionist cause was just around the corner, but they needed a workforce to help.

My father answered the Zionist call. Perhaps it fed his hunger for comradery and connection, or perhaps it gave him a purpose and a new place to call home. Whatever the case, he prepared to go to Palestine while learning Hebrew, studying Jewish history and culture, and memorizing songs about the homeland that he would sing for years to come.

Later, after serving in the military, he began studying at Mikveh Israel, the first Jewish agricultural school, located in Tel Aviv. The school's name means "Hope of Israel." Its goal was to train young agronomists and then send them throughout Israel so that wherever they settled it would be as if a spring had materialized to water the dry places. Through their bourgeoning families and agrarian development work, these young people would establish Israel and make it the Promised Land once more.

In 1949, after Israel had won the war of independence, my father was sent to work in Ein Kerem where, two years later, he encountered my mother at Mary's Spring. They were very different people. She was dark, with brown hair and eyes that contrasted with his fair hair, suntanned skin, and blue eyes. She was a Sephardic Jew, a descendent of Jews who had long ago settled in the Iberian Peninsula but who had since dispersed into other regions such as North Africa, the Middle East, and Southeast Europe (including Bulgaria). The Sephardim, as these Jews were called, had unique traditions and customs, and they tended to be more secular than the Ashkenazi Jews, to which my father belonged. The Ashkenazim descended from Jews who settled in Germany or thereabouts and eventually became known as the Jews from Eastern Europe. Like my father and his family, the Ashkenazim tended to be lighter skinned and more connected to their Jewish roots.

Despite their differences, my mother and father did not take long to marry. They never talked with me about what initially drew them to each other, but they were not the only seemingly mismatched couple to get married in Israel at that time. Many people from different regions and backgrounds had been thrown together in the melting pot of Israel and had chosen to start families quickly. Perhaps they sought the stability of marriage, or perhaps it was the passions of youth. One unquestionable factor was that, everywhere they turned, Zionism was beseeching them to settle, marry, and have babies. There was work to be accomplished and Israel's legitimacy to be established. The worldwide Jewish population had just taken a devastating blow. People were desperate and resolved to bring new life into the decimated nation.

After my parents married, my mother moved into the house that my father had claimed two years prior. They worked hard to make it a home. They put down roots in Ein Kerem. When I arrived within the year, they bestowed on me the name of the grandmother I would never meet: Bracha.

Our name means "a blessing."

CHAPTER FIVE

BECOMING

I did not need my father to tell me how it felt to be branded—both socially and physically—because I could run my finger over the number 19064 tattooed on his left forearm and feel the sting myself. Nor did my mother have to describe how it felt to have her life pulled out from under her; I could sense the bitterness that simmered beneath her words and actions. I did not need my father to tell me that he ached for his family; the discreet tears he shed during the Kaddish prayer of mourning spoke loud enough. And I did not need my mother to explain how the trauma of her past had changed her outlook on the future; I could detect her dampened spirit, the cloud that perpetually shadowed her heart.

Every morning, I saw my parents get up early to begin the unglamorous work of crafting a life from scratch. My father would eat his breakfast and head off to a long day of tilling the soil and imparting knowledge to his students. My mother, meanwhile, stayed busy managing mundane details at home. She was not expressive in her love or affection, but she demonstrated these sentiments through never-ending acts of service and a knack for creating culinary masterpieces out of simple ingredients.

I grew up with a profound feeling of indebtedness toward my parents. This instilled in me a growing desire—perhaps a burden—to make them proud of me. It was easy to please my father. Despite all he had been through, he was exceedingly cheerful and quick to laugh. He had a gift for making strangers feel like they were his new best friends. However, he reserved his true affections for his family.

"Proud of you?" he would laugh. "Proud is not strong enough a word! You're my little girl! You only had to breathe to make me fall in love with you! Nothing you do could make me happier than simply knowing I'm your Abba."

I knew my father meant every word, but I did not want to be complacent. I was always looking to make him prouder and happier. If he laughed when I was silly, I would act sillier. If he bragged about me in front of his friends, I would turn up the charm. Knowing that his face would light up when I told him about my school achievements, I always aimed to bring home the highest marks. If he gave me praise when I helped Eema around the house, I would find ways to go above and beyond. To be both the source and beneficiary of his delight was my highest aim.

My mother, however, was not so easy to satisfy. She was a good mother, but not a happy one. Resentment and self-pity flowed in her veins. Eema was not a weak-willed woman, but her soul was always downtrodden. I could not understand why she seemed so determined to be unhappy. This left me feeling confused about my mother's love. I sometimes wondered if I might be the source of her unhappiness. After all, my father had endured extreme suffering, yet he had proven to be far more resilient than her, and he always treated me with a father's joyful love.

Witnessing my parents' distinct responses to hardships over many years led me, later in life, to question where inner strength comes from, and why some people have it and others do not. But in my early years, I often wondered whether my mother's emotional distance meant that something was wrong with me. This concern affected nearly every interaction I had with her. Ultimately, I concluded that she bore no ill will toward me, but I often wished that she would be more affectionate and communicative. I longed for a life in which I came home from school, dropped my books on the kitchen table, and sprang into Eema's arms for a hug. I wanted her to set aside her chores, sit down beside me, and converse about the day. I wanted to tell her about my favorite teacher, about the games I had played with friends, about a classmate's mean comment. I wanted her, in turn, to tell me about her trip to the food stall, about the eccentric neighbor lady, or about how she had helped Savta that day. I imagined laughing with her like I did with my father. Sadly, my mother and I seemed to speak different languages.

Occasionally, Eema would snap and say something critical or unkind. When this happened, my sister often responded by lashing out or taking tearful refuge in her room. I, on the other hand, became strategic. Retreat was not an option, but neither was retaliation. Instead, I found other ways to combat her negativity: an apology, artificial lightheartedness, offering an optimistic alternative, doing extra chores. One of the easiest ways to make her happy was to cook with her or enthusiastically eat what she had made.

My mother's entire family loved food. For them, cooking and eating were not merely about health and sustenance. Food was about art, history, and a way to offer and receive love. I embraced this perspective wholeheartedly. One of my greatest joys was watching my mother's deft fingers as she sliced zucchini or sprinkled spices into a pot. She seemed to know instinctively which flavors would blend well. I observed in amazement as she transformed ordinary ingredients into dishes bursting with color and zest. In the kitchen my mother seemed to relax and release her instinctive strengths. For this reason, our kitchen, along with the tastes and aromas created there, became a haven for me.

Food was the one language my mother and I could share. If I asked for a double portion, she would beam with appreciation. And so, in part to connect with her, I overindulged. And that led to weight gain. This fact did not bother me when I was little. In fact, far from feeling insecure, I walked around with an innocent belief that I was adorable; after all, every adult I met had told me so! As I got older, however, the neighborhood kids increasingly excluded me because they did not like to play with "fat girls." It became worse as I moved up in grades. Girls who had claimed to be my friends began to make snide-but-subtle comments about my weight. Boys were less measured in their observations and critiques. I was a highly social child, so every relational rift hurt deeply. To hide my feelings, I would laugh and pretend that I had not heard the insult, or I would stoically act as if the sideways look or cutting remark had not hurt me.

When I shared these situations with my mother, she always came to my defense with encouraging words, but she also consoled me with food, which only provided momentary comfort. My father, on the other hand, was never my confidante in this matter. He would have been willing to help, but I wanted to shield our relationship from problems. With him I wanted everything to be, all the time, happy and uncomplicated. When we were together, I deftly buried my troubles and insecurities so that nothing sad or shameful could tarnish what we had between us.

Academics became a refuge. I often thought, *If I can't be the prettiest, I can at least be the sweetest and smartest.* I loved school, mostly because of the social interaction, but as friends began to reject me, I focused increasingly on my grades. I found comfort in the neat rows of desks, the pencils sharpened to fine points, and the immaculately dressed teachers. Whereas social relations with my peers seemed inconsistent and arbitrary, the adult world of learning appeared structured and steady. I thrived on the formulaic nature of it all. If I was polite with adults and asked intelligent questions in class, if my homework was turned in on time and complete, if I paid attention and worked diligently, then the teachers would always praise me. I could control the outcome.

From ages six to ten, I attended the school in Ein Kerem. It was a good school, but it was small like our village. I started to long for more rigorous academic challenges. When a neighbor friend told me that her parents had enrolled her in a prestigious school in Jerusalem where they taught, I began to dream about joining her.

Going to school in Jerusalem! I could hardly picture anything more glamorous. Our family had taken trips into the city many times, and I was enamored with the drama and commotion of its streets. Despite my love for Ein Kerem, I had become increasingly bored by its unhurried pace and quotidian routines. I had often begged my parents to move to Jerusalem (to no avail), but this time, because it involved a good school, I had higher hopes.

To my excitement, my parents thought it was a good idea. My father recognized that the school in Jerusalem was more academically advanced than the one in Ein Kerem and my mother was satisfied by the practicality of the plan. The new school was only thirty minutes by bus from our house. If I was accepted, they told me, I could go.

Determined to make my dream a reality, I sought out my friend's parents for assistance. They worked at the school, so I figured they would know what I should do to get in. They warned me that securing an interview and passing that stage would be a significant challenge. Undeterred, I asked if they would help. Something about my passion and persistence must have moved them because before long I was sitting in front of the school's principal and presenting my case. After asking me a battery of questions and patiently listening to my responses, he stood up, shook my hand, and officially invited me to study at the school.

On the first day of classes, I was up before dawn. I found my uniform neatly pressed and folded on top of my dresser. I slipped it on as butterflies clamored in my belly. After a quick breakfast and a peck on each cheek from Abba and Eema, I walked to the nearby bus stop in the early morning light. The winding road that climbed from Ein Kerem to Jerusalem and the people who made the bus trip alongside me would soon become very familiar. But on that morning, everything felt fresh and new.

Upon arrival at the school, I was enthralled. The ethnic and economic mix of students was just as diverse as my school in Ein Kerem, but I had never seen so many kids in one place. Instead of encountering the same friends and neighbors at school, I now swam in an ocean of new relational possibilities. The teachers were smart and interesting, and academically more demanding. Determined to exceed their expectations, I was always on time, never disrespectful, and consistently attentive during class. My teachers liked me, and I liked them.

Directly after school each day, I would go with one or more friends to my house or theirs where we would dutifully complete homework and share a snack. As younger siblings squealed and squawked, we would silently huddle around sheets of paper and scribble away. I loved being known as "the studious one." Here in our homes and away from peer pressure, my classmates were friendly and uncomplicated, often asking me for help when they got stuck. We would talk and laugh between mathematics problems, or we would read our essays to each other while we eagerly waited to be called to supper.

Acceptance from peers came and went, but I knew I could win the consistent friendship and praise of teachers by doing well in school—and that is what mattered most to me. Some teachers indicated that I had the potential to work in a high-status job as an adult. When they asked, I would tell them I wanted to be a doctor—because I knew that would impress them. In fact, I had no idea what I wanted to do when I grew up. I only knew that I wanted to make Israel proud. How could I do otherwise? Everywhere I turned, I was reminded subtly and overtly that I belonged to an extremely small, unique group—a generation who had been *born* as Israeli citizens. Being a Sabra was an honor, but it was also a weighty responsibility. At school, it drove me to perform and achieve.

Whereas some students found their passion or niche in a specific subject or skill, I spread my efforts across many subjects, never delving deeper than it took to win a good grade. I signed up for every extra-curricular activity that would fit into my schedule. Cooking, sewing, ceramics, choir—all provided opportunities to show that I could be good at everything.

My favorite subjects, however, were the ones that made me feel more connected to Israel and its history. Geography was one such class. Our teachers insisted that we, as inheritors of the new nation, must know its every ridge and region. With winsome words they reminded us that the land beneath our feet was the same land that our biblical ancestors had walked—a country of palm and olive trees, of pomegranates and figs, of arid deserts and rushing rivers. Books, maps, and posters gave us the necessary head knowledge about Israel's landscape and physical boundary lines, but it was the field trips that rooted our hearts in the soil. We went on nature hikes during which we "discovered" plants or insects and placed them in jars or documented them in journals to be shared later with the class. We visited farms and vineyards where we learned about irrigation and crops. A kibbutz was occasionally on the agenda. With sand in our shoes and dirt under our nails, we came to know and fall in love with our homeland. It seemed unthinkable that our parents would one day hand it off to us, but we knew it would be our responsibility to make this desert bloom.

In school I also enjoyed studying the Hebrew scriptures and the Talmud, a collection of Jewish history, laws, and ethics. For some, these ancient writings were dry and boring, but I lapped up the old stories, excited to find how many had occurred in the same locations we had discussed in geography class. The wilderness in the Sinai Peninsula where the Israelites had wandered for forty years was the same location where, just a few years earlier, our fathers had fought in the war of Israel's independence. It felt surreal to see the regions where my ancestors had settled match those featured on bus stops and local travel brochures. I considered it a matter of pride that Jerusalem, the City of David, was just a thirty-minute bus ride from home.

The stories enraptured me more than the geography, in part because my teachers made them come alive. I found that the Hebrew scriptures, known by

Christians as the Old Testament, addressed every topic, situation, question, or human experience. There was something solemn and exhilarating about opening the pages and contemplating the wisdom that had been passed down for generations. For me, the Talmud was even better. It expounded on the truths of the Old Testament in the form of orderly, precise proverbs. In class, we analyzed the Talmud until we had mastered its key lessons. We engaged in intensely gratifying and invigorating debates. I loved to dissect ideas and was fascinated by perspectives other than my own. Issues that at first seemed black and white were in fact beautifully complex.

These debates, proverbs, and truths satisfied my longing to see the world as rational and methodical. When boiled down, they told me that if I could be a good person, then I would be blessed. If I worked hard, I would be successful. If I was kind to others, I would be treated fairly. Each proverb seemed like an absolute formula, and that gave me great confidence. I just needed to follow the proper procedures. If I could do that, life would work out perfectly.

CHAPTER SIX

IMAGE

No matter how much we try to deny it, a hallmark of adolescence is the pressure to craft a persona that will be accepted by peers. I did my best to appear as though I had risen above such concerns, but my teen years were no less marked by this pressure.

Being a Sabra influenced the way I came to portray myself. Israel was about my age, a teenage nation. I grew up at a time when Israel was rebelling against the false image of the "weak and wretched" diaspora Jew. As the Israeli sociologist, historian, and painter Oz Almog wrote in 1997, "The Sabra was educated to see himself as the opposite of the stereotypical diaspora Jew—as belonging to a better breed of Jews, as a prince of the new Israeli kingdom. He was imbued with the sense that history had assigned him a decisive role in the realization of utopia."

I had received this type of education as child, and I felt pride in my Sabra identity, but at that time I believed my responsibility to Israel would only begin in some distant, exhilarating future. By the time I was a teenager, however, I began to feel a mounting pressure to live up to the Sabra ideal. I knew that my generation, the first generation in millennia to *not* be born in diaspora, would be responsible for establishing Israel's new national identity. It would be up to us to present an authentic view of Israel's, dignity, vivacity, and indomitability.

Shaping this new image of the "ideal Israeli" involved internal changes (heart and mind) and external changes (physical appearance). Regarding the latter, the model Israeli man would have stereotypically "gentile" features. The textbook Sabra male was described by Almog as "slender, lithe, sturdy, suntanned, and tall, with a long neck, a head crowned with hair, high cheekbones, a turned-up nose (not what the anti-Semites called a 'Jewish nose'), and a clean-shaven face with Slavic contours (the beard being a Jewish trademark)." This physique, especially when clothed in agrarian or military attire, would represent the new Israeli male archetype. No longer would he be imagined as bookish, frail, and passive. Instead, he would be seen as youthful, rugged, and self-confident.

As for the ideal Israeli woman, she would undergo more complicated changes. On the one hand, women admired the beauty of the *halutzah,* the Pioneer woman who had answered the Zionist call, left diaspora behind, and now spent her life in steadfast service to Israel. She was often portrayed as a suntanned, athletically built woman in modest clothing who worked alongside men in the fields or who trained in the Women's Corps of the IDF. This romanticized feminine ideal portrayed a glorified "natural" beauty, physical sturdiness, and material asceticism. To care too much about one's looks was frowned upon.

When I was growing up, however, this *halutzah* definition of beauty was beginning to succumb to Western ideals. Modesty and service were still high values, but women were beginning to be encouraged to accentuate femininity and put more effort into physical appearance. Women were to conduct themselves with the strength and integrity of a *halutzah* but *look* like a Sabra.

Despite the focus on external appearance, all Sabras knew that the foundation of the ideal Israeli was internal character. Emotional vitality, exuberance, and fortitude were far more important than beauty or athleticism. To be physically frail was frowned upon, but to be labeled *emotionally* frail was even worse. Such weakness would imply that we could not cope with life's harsh realities, that we were not capable of being *survivors.* Such a label was deplorable and embarrassing. Weakness, we were told, was antithetical to being an Israeli.

To prove our Sabra-ness, men and women of my generation had to steer clear of negativity and self-pity. If we were overly serious, it would imply a problematic melancholy. Israeli men, Almog points out, were most admired when they displayed their "lovable, playful, cunning, rough-hewn, anti-establishment character . . . [their] youthful charm and grinning sociability." Women were praised when they showed themselves to be "proud . . . independent and rebellious—like a symbol of that native generation of the homeland."

As a teenager, I was not thinking about these shifting ideals, but I perceived a subtle pressure to look and act like a Sabra. My father's resilient approach to life—he was the epitome of the Sabra ideal—encouraged me in that direction. My mother, who was emotionally volatile and always felt sorry for herself, was the antithesis of the ideal. Thus, the contrasting but deep influence of each parent in my life presented me with a choice between two ways of living. I came to believe that the Sabra ideal was the *right way to live.*

What I could not see then was that both of my parents embodied an extreme. I resented my mother's way of life and adored my father's, but I realized later that my father often presented an external image of strength to hide his human weaknesses. My mother's victim mentality had deprived her of contentment and joy, but my father's reluctance to share his sadness or talk about his trauma sometimes made him seem less authentic.

I would not realize these truths until later in life. As a teenager, I was more concerned with conforming to the new ideal for Sabras than with what that ideal might cost me. I believed that I needed to have it all: strength, intelligence, promise, and beauty. For a time, I felt like I was making progress toward that ideal. I had my father's positivity and emotional fortitude. I had good grades and the praise of teachers. I also had a respectable plan for my future, one that would bring honor to my parents and my country: serve in the military, go to college, get married, and establish a career—all while having a big family . . . six kids, at least!

When it came to beauty, I believed I fell short. My father always called me his "beautiful girl," but my peers still, on occasion, made unkind comments about my weight. I struggled with teenage self-scrutiny. I loved fashion and was always well-dressed, but I still felt shame whenever I looked in the mirror. As a Sabra with emotional fortitude, intelligence, and promise, I tried to suppress these vain thoughts. I worked hard to excel in school and tried to be a kind, likeable young woman. I did not want anyone to know that I was incredibly unhappy with my appearance.

Then a clothing shop in Jerusalem changed my life.

At age sixteen, I began taking a detour between school and the bus stop. The new walking route took me past a small fashion boutique with clean windows and bright signage. As I passed, I always stopped to peer through the windows at the racks of beautiful clothes and elegant outfits on mannequins. The women who walked out with shopping bags hanging from their wrists all looked so sleek and charming! Everything about the store seemed magical.

As I rode the bus home each evening, I visualized myself wearing the clothes I had seen through the shop window. In my imagination, some clothing made me look refined and some made me look sassy, but each garment seemed to have the power to transform my plump, schoolgirl form into a beautiful woman's. Perhaps, I mused, clothing could fill what had been missing in my life.

One sunny Saturday, I took the bus to Jerusalem and wandered the busy sidewalks while my mother shopped at the market. I had some money but no intention of spending it. Ambling down the main streets and dodging other pedestrians on the busy sidewalk, I suddenly found myself walking by the same shop that had captured my attention for weeks. The door was open to welcome fresh air and passersby.

Why not just look? I thought.

This simple decision, at that point in my life, took courage. Prior to that day, whenever my mother had taken me shopping for clothes, I had become anxious about my appearance. To enter a dressing room with mirrors all around, to know that I would have to model each outfit for my mother, to wonder what all the other women in the store thought about my appearance—the whole ordeal had filled me with cold dread. But on that day, before I knew it, I was inside the store and clutching several outfits to my chest. A sales associate guided me to the back and pointed me to a dressing room. She smiled kindly before drawing the curtain behind me.

I was alone, but those old feelings of embarrassment and dread returned. I hung the clothes on a hook beside me and examined them once again. I pictured myself walking into my classroom wearing them, and I imagined the flash of jealousy on the girls' faces as the boys stared at me.

I unzipped the back of the first dress, a dress that I had coveted for weeks, while imagining that it would help me win the heart of some studious, handsome boy at school. I even envisioned that the boy would give me my first kiss at the garden gate outside my house.

That daydream quickly evaporated. I drew the dress up and felt it stop at my hips.

I knew it. Why did I even try?

Then fury, or something like it, overtook my feelings of embarrassment. I realized that I was sick of being ashamed about my appearance. I was fed up with my ill-fitting clothes. I stepped back and took a hard look at myself in the mirror. It was uncomfortable, but I forced myself to not look away. I noted every imperfection and roll that I had always tried to hide. Finally, I stepped forward and looked into my eyes. It felt as if I was staring down one of my bullies.

"No more," I whispered. "I'm done with this."

I left the shop, not with a new wardrobe, but with determination. Self-pity and despair would no longer define me. I had decided to change. And I did.

⚜

Channeling my father's strong will and my mother's pragmatism, I immediately ended my unhealthy eating habits and placed myself on a strict but healthy diet, improving the nutritional quality and reducing the quantity of the food I ate. I abandoned nuts, butter, rice, potatoes, bread, fried foods, and desserts. I began eating more fruits, vegetables, and lean meats. This healthy eating plan was self-generated and self-enforced. The first weeks were the hardest, not because I was starving or feeling ill, but because I craved the less healthy foods that had been part of my normal habits.

I had not informed any adults, not even my father, about my resolute decision to lose weight, but they could see that I had become more selective in my food choices, and they could see the gradual weight loss. In hindsight, I should have told them, but at the time I did not want them to thwart my efforts. The lack of information, of course, made my mother worry. At first, she remained silent while looking at the unfinished food on my plate. Sometimes she would glare at me disapprovingly. Before long she became critical and angry.

"Eat! Why aren't you eating!" she would scold.

I would tell her that I was not hungry, or that I was feeling a little sick, or that I had already eaten with friends. My mother saw right through me. She had never known me to be rebellious, so she began to speculate, superstitiously, that I had been cursed by the "evil eye" or some other spirit. Then, despite my healthy appearance, her tendency to worry about everything led her to think that I might have some disease. That unwarranted fear was fueled by the fact that one of my cousins had died. She thought I might be destined for the same fate.

As tensions heated up between us, I did my best to assuage my mother's worries. When she came to my room ranting about my diet, I tried to assure her that I was not sick or starving, that in fact I was healthier than before. Despite my efforts, she was not content with my explanations. Food, after all, had always been the primary means through which my mother had shown me love, and her kitchen was the one place where she could be the mother she aspired to be. Her love for us had been infused into her dishes along with the herbs and spices. My resolve must have felt to her like rejection, but I remained resolute. I knew I was not in danger and that I was not harming anyone, not even my mother.

Self-discipline continued to produce results. Clothes began to feel looser. Muscle definition began to emerge. In a matter of months, I arrived at the healthy weight I had set out to achieve. I felt like a woman. Others seemed to agree.

"Someone lost her baby face!" my neighbors would say. "What a beautiful girl you've turned out to be!"

"Smart *and* pretty!" my teachers would say.

After years of being criticized and teased about my weight, the attention and compliments were flattering. My self-confidence began to climb. When gym class rolled around twice a week, I no longer battled anxiety or begged my father for a note of excuse. Boys started saying nice things to me, and more girls wanted to be my friend. Everything, I felt, was headed in the right direction. Most importantly, the weight-loss effort had reinforced my appreciation for living according to formulas. By setting a goal, making a plan, and exerting self-discipline to reach a target, I could transform my life.

CHAPTER SEVEN

MISS ISRAEL

As a young girl and during my early teen years, I had seen myself as a helpless victim of unfortunate genes, a person destined to always be heavy. But losing weight enabled me to see that I did not need to be defeated by these negative thoughts. I could take control of my life. This exciting lesson would help me when I turned eighteen and began military training.

Since 1948, Israel has been one of the few nations in the world to draft both men and women into military service. Women had fought in combat during the war for independence, but when I joined in 1970 we were only allowed to serve as office workers, nurses, and instructors. Even so, we in the Women's Corps were expected to undergo the same rigorous combat training as the men.

Today, the IDF allows women to occupy nearly all the same military roles as men. In 2006, it even created the first company of all-female combat soldiers in the world—the Nachshol Reconnaissance Company. With their fatigues, combat boots, and berets, today's female IDF members are barely distinguishable from their male counterparts. In 1970, men and women wore the same clothing during training, but as soon as we entered the military workforce, the women received a feminine khaki skirt and blouse.

Military service will unavoidably influence a woman's self-perception, her deepest understanding of what it means to be female. The uniforms are basically masculine—baggy fatigues, heavy boots, backpacks—and the drills are anything but delicate. In my case, the rigorous physical demands and aggressive combat training developed inner strength. It toughened my heart, mind, and body.

I had joined the IDF with excitement and trepidation—thrilled to be a part of my nation's military and contribute to something bigger than myself, but nervous about whether I could prove my mettle. Prior to my arrival at training, I had lost weight, but I was not physically fit. I was a girl who had often skipped gym class. I had never jogged a mile or done a single sit-up.

Military training is designed, among other things, to be a crucible. No one escapes the process without being broken down and then rebuilt as a soldier. In the IDF, our unrelenting instructors wanted us to be able to survive in the harshest conditions and to have unbreakable spirits. They wanted to prepare us for the tragic possibility of dying for our country. Some days it *felt* like we were dying. Our instructors pushed us to our limits and into states of misery. The early morning bugle calls, the strenuous exercises, the agonizing midnight marches—everything taught us that during training we could no longer avoid suffering. We were going to be IDF soldiers, the men and women called to defend a tiny nation surrounded by less-than-friendly countries, so we might as well get comfortable with discomfort.

Over time, my fellow unit members and I found the physical and mental stamina we needed. We learned to bound out of bed when the morning wakeup call sounded—always sooner than expected. During intense fitness exams, I learned to focus my thoughts on anything other than my body. When ordered to jump from an airborne plane, I learned to overcome my natural fear and trust the equipment and training I had received.

Our broad and intense training involved wilderness survival skills, marksmanship, parachuting, and desert navigation. We hiked countless miles under the blazing sun and during the dead of night. Through it all, I learned the importance of unity and teamwork. I learned that by persevering through extreme hardship I could expand the definition of "possible."

At the end of training, I was an official Israeli soldier—not just in name, but in my heart. I felt proud to belong Israel's military and to my community of soldier women. The IDF training had given me confidence that I could fulfill my childhood desire to be a Sabra, to uphold the legacy and reputation of previous generations. The experience reshaped my view of womanhood.

During my first days in the military, I felt like a lost and lonely little girl. Nothing was familiar. There was no Abba or Eema close by, no kitchen table piled high with schoolwork. I had entered a new, unknown life. But I gradually formed friendships, especially with female soldiers who shared my interest in dancing and singing. As teenagers, a few of us had been involved in choirs and school plays, so we all harbored visions of fame. While whispering across the gap between our cots, I discovered that some of them had hoped (like me) to be selected for an IDF military ensemble.

These ensembles comprised servicemembers who, instead of training to become mechanics, medics, or combat soldiers, used their creative talents to serve Israel. They still participated in typical soldierly tasks, but their focus was on singing, dancing, acting, and music.

For those of us who loved to sing and act, my friends and I could not imagine a military career more suited to our interests and aspirations. Many performers had achieved stardom because of their reputations in the ensembles. When training got tough, my bunkmate and I fantasized about a future with record deals, red carpets, and world tours.

Girlish fantasies came to an end when our career placements were announced and I learned that I would be sent to Tel Aviv to work as a secretary. It was an unwelcome disappointment, but I had become an IDF soldier, sworn to serve the needs of the military wherever that might lead.

I dreaded saying goodbye to my fellow soldiers. Basic training had been the most difficult experience of my life, but I had found comfort in its routine and structure. Even our tent had become dear to me, a home away from home populated by tough women who had eased the ache of being far from family. Soon, I would be on my own again.

After the rigorous training that I had just endured, the thought of being a secretary seemed terribly boring, but a superior officer told me that I would be stationed in the IDF general headquarters, in the same building as the IDF's chief of staff. My job would be to provide vital support to a commander, one of Israel's greatest strategic minds, Avraham Tamir. I would also be working around some of the country's most influential military men.

"You're a pretty girl," the officer added. "And headquarters is full of crotchety old men. You will brighten the place up. Give the whole place a makeover."

After months of wearing fatigues and enduring the daily shouts of my instructors, it caught me off guard to be called pretty. As I thought about my future work, I wondered if the traditionally female aspects of my nature might reemerge. I also wondered how the physical and psychological strength I had gained during training could possibly be sustained in a secretarial role. There was not much time to dwell on these matters, but the other women at headquarters and I often laughed about the disconnect between our training and our jobs. Instead of jumping out of planes, we clambered on and off crowded city buses. Instead of loading and shooting firearms, we tinkered with staplers. And that navigational course we took in the Sinai Desert? A compass was not needed to locate the desk of a commanding officer.

At times I also felt intellectually underutilized, but the secretarial job was stimulating in other ways. Our office hummed with activity and always required a high degree of order and efficiency. I soon met many of the nation's leading diplomats, politicians, and military advisors. I was proud to contribute, even in a small way, to the work they were doing for our nation. Whenever I called home, my father would bombard me with questions.

"Who did you meet today?" he asked. "Was it the minister of foreign affairs?

A brigadier general? The prime minister, perhaps?"

"Nothing so grand," I replied. "But I did make a cup of coffee for Ariel Sharon this morning..."

"*General* Ariel Sharon?" my father asked.

I could not help gloating a little. I knew my father would give anything to meet Sharon, who had begun his illustrious military career in the Haganah.

"Around here we call him *Arik*," I teased, referring to Sharon's nickname. I also confessed that the general had flirted with me, adding that I had avoided a scene by jumping up to get him coffee.

"Well . . . well he can spill that coffee right down his trousers for all I care!" My father retorted. "That's all he'd better hope for from a sweet girl like you!"

My father had no reason to worry about *me*. Headquarters was obviously full of men, but plenty of women worked there, too. There were some concerning male-female office dynamics, but the women knew how to watch out for each other.

Batya, an older and wiser woman who reminded me of my grandmother, looked out for me. We soon became close.

"It's like the good teacher said," said Batya in reference to Jesus of Nazareth. "Behold, I send you forth as sheep in the midst of wolves . . .' Trust me, dear. Too many girls walk in here with their sweet little lamb eyes and end up in some brute's jowls! Wise as a serpent, harmless as a dove. That's what you need to be! What else do you think they mean when they say they 'decorate their officers'?"

Batya's warnings were not unwarranted. Most flirtation was harmless, but one could never be sure. She cautioned me and other women against arriving at work too early or staying too late. She did not want us to be left vulnerable in a nearly empty office. The men's attention could be flattering, but thanks to Batya, I kept up my guard. I became an expert at judging just how far I could go with my friendliness and prided myself for always "holding the reins" in my interactions with men. Reminded by Batya that "sweet" and "shrewd" were not mutually exclusive traits, I made sure to exercise both. I was pleasant and professional, but I refused to be some officer's "decoration."

It was also Batya who, a few months after I started working at IDF headquarters, offhandedly brought up the Miss Israel competition. We were eating our lunch in the break room when she briefly stared at me.

"You know, you are very beautiful."

I rolled my eyes. "You sound like my Savta, old woman!" Batya and I often teased each other, but instead of countering with a snide remark, she pressed on.

"No, I'm serious. I think you could do it," she said. "I think you could win!"

"What are you talking about?"

"The competition in Jerusalem. You should go! You'd show all those hyenas what real beauty is." Batya leaned back in her chair triumphantly, as if there was nothing more to discuss.

"Are you talking about the Miss Israel competition?" I asked hesitantly. I could not imagine what else she might mean.

"Of course! Miss Israel," she confirmed. "Women on the bus this morning were talking about it. Apparently, the organizers are about to choose contestants."

Batya was right. The night before, my roommate showed me a magazine article about that year's Miss Israel competition. It said that the search for contestants was underway. I failed to see how such news related to my life.

Once the break room conversation with Batya ended, the matter slipped my mind. However, a couple of weeks later, she arrived at the office waving a large white envelope in her wrinkled hand.

"I knew it!" she crowed. "I knew they would agree with me. You're an Esther among women!"

"Batya!" I interjected. "What did you do?"

"What do you think? I wrote those people in Jerusalem! I told them all about you, inside and out. And I said that they should not bother looking for other contestants because you would be sure to take the crown!"

There was no hiding my surprise. Batya had actually signed me up for the Miss Israel competition. As I wondered how she had managed to apply without my knowledge, she walked toward me and thrust an envelope into my hands.

"I know that you're wondering how I finished the application without you. It wasn't easy, but don't worry. My letter of recommendation was flawless. The application required some forgery, though."

"Forgery? What does the letter say?" I asked as a few women from the office gathered around.

"Open it and see," one of them urged. Apparently, they had all known about Batya's secret.

I slipped the letter out of the envelope and skimmed the first line, which thanked me for applying to participate in the 1971 Miss Israel pageant. I read further. It said that I had been selected out of hundreds of applicants to progress to the interview stage in Tel Aviv.

Batya, who had impatiently read the letter upon receipt, was beside herself. "All hail the beauty queen of Israel!"

The next few months passed in a blur. For Batya's sake, I agreed to go through the interview phase. I started with indifference, but I became more enthusiastic as I learned more about the preliminary process. Contestants would spend months being groomed for the competition, and they would be lavished with gifts from sponsors. The nationally broadcast pageant would be hosted by Israel's greatest TV and radio celebrities. After the competition, they said, Miss Israel, Miss Jerusalem, and the runners-up would have months of modeling contracts and press opportunities. For a girl who had always pored over fashion magazines and dreamed of performing in front of a crowd, the pageant seemed increasingly alluring.

After finishing the interview stage, I received a large brown envelope with a note of congratulations. I had qualified to participate in the televised competition. The envelope included an outline of the pre-pageant schedule. The next morning, I discreetly deposited the packet on Batya's desk and told her that I had been selected to be among twenty-two constestants. Batya's shriek of triumph was the subject of lunchroom banter for weeks. So was the news that I would be competing for the Miss Israel crown.

The pageant's second phase was even busier than the first, all of which had to be managed while continuing to fulfill my duties at IDF headquarters. Over the next four months, all finalists had to be taught the proper way to walk, talk, sit, and stand. We were taxied around to various vendors so that we could select our competition outfits. There were photoshoots, fancy dinners, and copious amounts of free samples and gifts. We received coaching on hair and makeup styles, practiced for the talent and interview segments, and rehearsed every smile and movement until we could have done it all in our sleep. Still, none of it seemed real until I picked up a popular women's magazine and found my name and headshot featured in a spread about the contestants.

The attention was flattering, but as the day of the pageant drew near, I felt like I was living two separate lives: one as a dutiful IDF servicemember from a simple village and the other as a pampered beauty contestant. This tension caused me to wonder again about what it meant to be a woman. I enjoyed the glamor for a while, but I wanted to be recognized for more than my outward appearance. The pageant was supposed to showcase intelligent, accomplished, and beautiful women, but the emphasis clearly fell on physical appearance. I worried about what my parents, especially my father, thought about me and my decision to participate. Pageantry did not seem to fit with the Sabra ideal.

The moment a person jumps out of a plane, there is no return. Likewise, when the day of the contest arrived, there was no turning back. A huge crowd had gathered at Jerusalem's International Convention Center. Seven contestants were active IDF members, so the audience included a disproportionate number of supporters from the military community. The atmosphere backstage was charged with nervous energy.

Bathed in bright light, the other contestants and I sat in high-backed chairs as attendants labored to perfect our hair and makeup. We tried to stay calm, or at least to conceal our anxiety. Some relied on contrived elation. Others, on false modesty.

"Well girls, we made it!" said one of the more boisterous women. "In just a couple hours one lucky lady will officially be Miss Israel!"

"I'm not even sure how I got here," said another demurely. "You all are so much prettier. I feel like I might as well go home now!" The room erupted with protestations and consolations.

As the evening proceeded, my nervousness was eclipsed by disgust . . . at myself. I wondered how I had allowed myself to become so self-absorbed. I looked around the room and felt profoundly disconnected from the rest of the women. Unlike those with whom I had bonded during basic training, none of these women had become dear to me. I did not fault them. The problem was mine to own. I had allowed myself to be carried along by vanity. I was in it for myself, not to be part of a team or a higher cause. In that moment, I thought of my mother and the other women like her in Ein Kerem. Rarely had that generation of women enjoyed such luxury. They had been too busy making unsung personal sacrifices for the greater good of Israel.

The thought made me feel foolish. Here I was about to stand in front of a national audience and be scrutinized, in large part, for my appearance. Crowns and sashes would be bestowed on four of us—the Beauty Queen of Israel, the Beauty Queen of Jerusalem, and their two runners-up—simply because we had been born with long legs and symmetrical faces.

As I thought about my family waiting outside, I had the urge to flee the dressing room and find them. It had been weeks since I had talked on the phone with my father, and I worried that he might think I had become frivolous. As I looked in the mirror, I could hardly bear the thought. I knew I could not reconcile my involvement in the pageant with the woman I desired to become, a woman who placed family and country ahead of fame and frivolity. But I had already jumped out of this plane. There was no turning back.

The show began. I was amazed by the efficiency and polish of it all. Backstage we were primed for each section of the program. Hairstylists, cosmetic specialists, and wardrobe assistants made everything happen rapidly. As we stepped into the bright lights and applause, the stage managers reminded us to smile wide and concentrate on our elegant walks.

Hosting the show was Israeli celebrity Yehoram Gaon, a singer and film actor who had been launched into stardom by serving in an IDF ensemble. The other contestants and I were excited to be near this famous man. His charm and professionalism made our job easy as the competition's rounds whizzed by. We posed in various outfits—casual, formal gown, sporty, bathing suit, and others—and demonstrated our talents. I sang a song about Israel that my father had taught me as a girl. My smile was genuine because I imagined him humming along from somewhere in the audience. Finally, we entered the final phase: the interviews.

These were conducted by the famous TV news presenter Haim Yavin. With microphone in hand, I answered Yavin's questions about my hometown, my interests, and what I did when I was not competing for Miss Israel. When I said that I was about a year into my service in the IDF, the crowd erupted with whoops and cheers; after all, the audience was inundated with rowdy military personnel. I was thankful for the support.

"So, young lady," Yavin asked. "What do you hope to do next? What do you want to pursue in the future?"

Forgetting whatever poised and sophisticated response I had planned, I unreservedly answered with the truth.

"I would like to go to college, get married, and have six children!"

Other women had given inspiring answers about lofty plans designed to impress the judges and please the audience. My down-to-earth answer caught everyone, including myself, off guard.

"Six children!" Yavin grinned as he looked across the audience. "You'd better get busy!"

More whoops, cheers, and laughter burst from the crowd. I laughed with them! The humorous moment dissolved the inner tension with which I had been struggling. I simply decided that it did not matter if I won or lost. I just wanted to contribute to Israel's betterment in ordinary ways, just as my parents had shown me. I wanted to complete my civic duty, get a good education, find an honorable man, and give my parents a house full of grandchildren.

Then the time came to announce the winners. To my surprise, I was brought forward as one of the final four. Outwardly delighted but inwardly torn, I accepted the "Miss Jerusalem Runner-Up" sash that Yehoram Gaon placed over my head.

That night I met up with my parents and was relieved to see that they were proud of me. They could hardly wait to return to Ein Kerem for local celebrations. I told them that the experience had clarified my vision for life. I would complete my post-pageant responsibilities while finishing my last year of military service. After that, I would go to college.

CHAPTER EIGHT

ZVI

The months following the Miss Israel contest were busy. Pageant sponsors wanted to leverage the publicity that our crowns and sashes offered, so after work each day, the other winners and I dutifully made appearances and modeled clothing. It was nice to have something to do with my free time and I enjoyed the fashionable attire, but when a photographer or two offered to line up modeling work for me outside of Israel, I declined. I did not want *anything* to get in the way of earning a college degree.

As the year wore on, my pageant schedule began to thin out and I was left with little or nothing to do in the evenings. The thought of relaxing at home was not appealing; there was too much to do, see, and eat in a bustling city like Tel Aviv. To avoid whiling away the hours until bed, I decided to join my coworkers and friends around tables at outdoor cafes. We talked and laughed for hours. Slow walks up and down the narrow streets of the Jaffa district or the Yemenite Quarter led us to hidden gems of architecture or cultural venues. Sometimes a few of us would make our way to the waterfront where we could sink our toes into the sand and watch the orange sun melt into the Mediterranean. I would inevitably think of my father and the sunset walks that had so long been part of our relational rhythm. I wondered if he missed me, or if he knew how much I yearned for his company.

Sometimes I felt lonely in the big city. Despite a steady stream of new people to meet, only a few had become good friends. As for the men, our paths would cross, we would talk and flirt, and then go our separate ways. These interactions offered temporary excitement, but they were exhausting. I sincerely wanted to build a meaningful life—a Sabra life—but every young man I met lacked the sturdy character I had hoped to find.

Frustrated and tired of trying to find a man with whom I could lay a foundation for life, I began to look for more productive ways to spend my evenings. I wanted to be useful, not frivolous. After some inquiring, I learned that a handful of my coworkers needed occasional childcare in the evenings. I offered my assistance. I liked the thought of serving a need while earning a little side income. Some coworkers, however, told me that I should combat boredom by going on more dates.

"We heard what you said in the pageant," they once said. "We know what you want. You don't need another job; you need a man who can give you those six babies!"

A few coworkers offered to set me up on blind dates. I usually agreed out of courtesy, but after each date I felt sure that I would not be settling down any time soon. The men were handsome and nice, but they approached relationships flippantly. It was hard for me to see the point.

"What do you expect?" some of the married women would ask. "They're young! You're young! Have some fun!"

Others warned me against being too picky. "If you don't settle down with one of these boys soon, you're going to miss your chance! Then what would your parents think?"

At age nineteen, I did not see any reason to be worried or be in a rush. My parents supported my desire to go to college before marriage. Besides, I believed the college setting would provide me with a better chance of meeting a good man, someone sincere and studious, dashing and debonair.

A friend set me up with a man named Yosi, an insurance agent by day and a flirtatious partygoer by night. We went on a few dates, but the relationship never blossomed into a romance, so we decided to be friends instead. As a sign of his goodwill, Yosi offered me an evening job helping him with office work. I accepted.

Yosi's office was in desperate need of order. On evenings when I was hard at work organizing, Yosi would come by to "help." He would swivel around in his office chair and talk to me, invariably beseeching me to wrap things up so he could treat me to dinner.

"I'm a starving, lonely bachelor!" he would say dramatically. "You're not going to turn me down, are you?"

We remained friends, and I always maintained an emotional distance between us. My time working in the IDF headquarters had taught me how to employ evasive tactics to fend off men's amorous advances. Yosi had always been respectful, but I remained on guard. My dating life was on hold.

One evening, Yosi strolled into the office with a handsome stranger.

"Bracha, I should have fired you a long time ago. I mean, look at the state of this place!" he said sarcastically. "But I knew I had to introduce you two first. Meet Zvi."

Yosi's friend Zvi surveyed the room as if inspecting my work. I noticed that he bore the telltale signs of military service: dark hair shorn close on the sides; wide, squared shoulders tapering down to a trim waist; strong stance; arms that rested in the "at-ease" position behind his back. This was no surprise, since most Israeli men my age had served in the IDF. What did surprise me was the way he looked at me. Many men I had met since the pageant had either self-consciously failed to look me in my eyes or had looked at me with cocky, possessive expressions. Zvi's smile was charming, but his eyes were neither arrogant nor shy. He looked at me with intelligence and poise.

"Zvi just came back from studying engineering abroad," said Yosi as Zvi shook my hand. "I told him he needed to have a little fun and experience the Tel Aviv nightlife!"

"Well, Yosi certainly knows how to show a person a good time," I said.

"That's what I told him," Yosi said. "But he always tells me that he'd rather do something more productive with his time. I told him it sounded like something you'd say, so he finally agreed to meet you."

"Yosi thinks that anyone who is more interested in work than flirting with girls every night must have something wrong with them," Zvi said, giving me a conspiratorial grin. "But hey, I'm not going to apologize for not being desperate. Maybe he should've picked something more interesting than insurance."

I couldn't help but laugh. Clearly, Zvi knew his friend well and was not afraid to point out the truth. Yosi *did* hate his job, and he *did* use girls and parties to distract himself from his discontent. I admired Zvi for not being embarrassed to call him out.

Yosi quickly changed subjects and started to jabber about how the two of them had met and where we might all go for dinner, drinks, and dancing. I kept glancing at Zvi. Whenever our eyes met—for some mysterious reason—I felt like we were old friends sharing an inside joke. Intrigued by our unspoken connection, I wished I had not promised a friend that I would babysit.

When I told him about my prior commitment, Yosi threw his hands up in mock exasperation. But Zvi, whose eyes had begun to meander around the office again, cut him off.

"A woman of valor, who can find?" he said.

His words came from the opening line of the *Eishet Chayil*, which is the passage about the "woman of valor" found in the Hebrew scriptures. Even today, Israeli men sing the Eishet Chayil to their wives before Shabbat dinner as a form of respect and praise. It defines the "ideal" woman, describing her as beautiful, strong like a soldier, competent in both household and business affairs, wise, and entrepreneurial. This ennobling and lofty ideal for women had long inspired me.

Zvi's reference caught me off guard, but he proceeded to quote more from the Eishet Chayil.

"She senses that her trade is profitable; her light does not go out at night."

I knew that he was flirting, but I was spellbound. Most guys defaulted to tacky jokes or complimenting my outfit.

"She looks after the conduct of her household and never tastes the bread of laziness," Zvi continued.

"Okay, listen," Yosi interrupted. "I'm too hungry to put up with you two geniuses talking in code. Let's go. I wouldn't mind tasting some 'bread of laziness' right about now."

Reluctantly, I insisted that I had to babysit that night, but I promised to be available for another outing soon.

Bicycles clattered by on the street as we stepped outside. A well-dressed couple walked briskly arm in arm. Having finished the workday, everyone was either heading home or to the city center for a fun night out. Everyone but me. I was wrapping up job number two for the day and heading to job number three. Yet, regarding Zvi, I had never felt so intrigued by a man at first encounter. Surely, I thought, my coworker would understand if my babysitting dependability lapsed just once.

Zvi, noticing my hesitation, interrupted decisively. "What are you doing tomorrow night? If I may, I'd like to swing by."

"That would be nice," I told him. "I'll be here tomorrow evening, same time."

I spent a few hours babysitting before making my way home. Zvi never left my mind. I found him to be confident but not arrogant, direct but not domineering, playful but not immature. I was most intrigued by the fact that he had compared me to the Eishet Chayil. That, I surmised, revealed a lot about him and what he was seeking in life. After all, the passage does not only depict a paragon of womanhood; it was also written for *men*, to help them set their standards high. Such a woman, it says, "is more precious than corals" and "brings him good, not harm, all the days of her life." The Eishet Chayil was an exhortation for men to treat women as rare and costly treasures. As I rested my head on my pillow that night, I remembered my lifelong desire to become a woman of valor. I hoped that Zvi saw that potential in me.

The next day I was back in Yosi's office, filing and fidgeting. I prolonged tasks, wanting to appear busy when Zvi arrived. As time wore on, I began to doubt that he would show up. I assumed he had met some other girl the previous night and had decided to go out with her instead, which would have been consistent with my recent dating experiences.

Finally, I gathered up my things and stepped outside to lock up the office. Descending the stairs to the sidewalk, my cynical thoughts were interrupted by a man's voice.

"Long day, huh?"

My head whipped up to see Zvi leaning, hands in his pockets, against a car parked against the curb. All my frustrations began to fade as I saw his roguish smile.

"You thought I forgot, didn't you?"

"Maybe," I conceded. "How long have you been out here? Why didn't you come in?"

"I peeked in the window but saw that you were busy, and I didn't want to interrupt. But you took so long you almost forced my hand. Are you ready to eat? I'm famished."

In one swift movement, Zvi pushed himself away from the car, flung the passenger door open, and began making his way to the driver's side. He offered no further invitation, no backward glance to see if I was following. It was as if he had picked me up like this a thousand times. He was not the most gentlemanly or romantic fellow, but there was something attractive about Zvi's sureness. He charged ahead in a way that made me want to follow. Before I had time to think, I was sitting his car and watching him turn the key. With that, we were off.

Our first date was indicative of Zvi's personality: fast-paced and intense. That night he drove me to the Jaffa district, treated me to a nice dinner, and walked with me around the Jaffa port where he promised to soon take me sailing. As stories and information energetically poured out of him, it became clear that Yosi had been right: Zvi *was* something of a genius. He possessed more than "book smarts." He was an experiential learner who lived life vigorously. At age twenty-four, only five years older than me, he had already become a captain in the IDF, been wounded in the Six Day War, traveled all over Israel and abroad, and acquired both a bachelor's degree and a master's degree in textile engineering. He was knowledgeable about many topics, including food, architecture, and local history; and he enjoyed many hobbies, such as sailing and woodworking. Despite his accomplishments and knowledge, he did not talk much about himself. Zvi curiously asked sincere questions about me and listened intently to my responses.

At the end of the night, Zvi dropped me off with a promise to be back the next evening.

"And, if you'll let me, the next and the next," he said with a smile.

After agreeing and saying goodnight, I climbed the stairs to my apartment. Something told me that my life would never be the same.

Sure enough, Zvi came back the next day and every day that followed. He proved to be an all-or-nothing man. He was not the type to settle for a romantic fling, nor was he one to hedge his bets or take it slow. Once he had me in his sights, he was anything but measured in the pursuit.

Zvi was exactly the kind of man that my parents had hoped I would marry. Aside from not being a native-born Israeli (he was born in Germany and his family had immigrated to Israel when he was three), he fit the Sabra ideal perfectly. He was strapping, handsome, and bold. He was intelligent and assertive, a risk-taker yet rational. His parents were successful entrepreneurs with a good name in the community, and they had raised their son to be a man of strong values and solid character.

Despite his qualities, Zvi was not everything *I* had dreamed of marrying. I had always pictured myself marrying someone more like my father. Both men shared a similar exuberance, but my father was easygoing, gentle, and relational, whereas Zvi could sometimes behave like a bulldozer. He was never malicious, but he acted with his head more than his heart. This worried me. I wondered if we could we be happy together, or if our differences would make us miserable.

Nevertheless, I could not deny his attributes. He was an open book. Black and white. A deep but uncomplicated thinker. I sometimes wished that he could be more romantic and tenderhearted, the kind of beau who might write me poetry or bring me flowers, but I also knew that such flourishes lacked substance when weighed against Zvi's character and commitment. He was frank, jovial, decisive, and dependable. He wouldn't fulfill all my dreams, but he would be forever loyal. I knew it.

"His *frame* is good," I told my friends.

"I'll say it is!" they joked.

I was not talking about his physique. When I looked at Zvi, I pictured a house. Maybe the house didn't have the precise layout I had originally envisioned, but it was made of good materials. Its foundation was solid, and its frame was secure. I could make a life there.

After three whirlwind weeks of dating, Zvi turned to me and casually asked, "Do you want to get married?" I looked at the promise in his eyes and said yes.

CHAPTER NINE

FORMULA FOR LIFE

C ultural norms in Israel at that time deemphasized "marrying for love" and encouraged people to marry young and have kids quickly, but I started to question whether I was making the right decision. Would we be happy? Would we realize after a few years that hormonal urges had suppressed wisdom? I knew that at age nineteen I was susceptible to being emotionally swept off my feet. I had seen young women follow romantic feelings only to find, when the fires of passion had subsided, that they were married to men without character. The *feeling* of love, I surmised, was flighty. Feelings alone would impair my judgment.

However, although Zvi and I cared about each other, our relationship was not founded on sentimentality. This meant that I was free to objectively assess Zvi and our relationship, unclouded by the fog of infatuation. What I saw was a man I could trust, a man whose mind and heart were aligned with my vision for life. Zvi likewise believed that he had found a woman of valor, one who would walk alongside him through life with "strength and dignity." In him, I found a force to be reckoned with, a man who would lead his family, provide, and remain committed forever. These traits would form the bedrock of a life in which happiness and affection could be cultivated over time. Pragmatism, not only passion, had driven us to get married.

This was the logic I had applied since my school days. Ancient books like Proverbs and the Talmud had told me that *wisdom* was the path to the "good life," and wisdom was like a formula. As a child, I lived as if life was an equation: work hard in school plus be kind to others equals wisdom. In my teenage years it had changed to a different equation: wisdom plus discipline equals a woman of valor. Now, it was this: a woman of valor plus a man "respected at the city gates" equals a successful marriage and family. On a broader level, a good life, I believed, included receiving a college education, establishing a profitable career, raising children, and contributing to Israel's future. It was an elaborate and ambitious equation, but with Zvi beside me I could see it all coming together.

Before marriage, however, I wanted to complete my military service. I was newly engaged and thus entitled to cut short my time in the IDF. Zvi, tired of his bachelor lifestyle and excited for the future, encouraged me to take advantage of this exemption.

"Just think," he would say. "We could elope and start our life together right away! You, me, a honeymoon in the north of Israel, then a place of our own here in Tel Aviv."

The thought was tempting. My office job had become mundane and wearisome, and life with four roommates was far from glamorous. Nevertheless, I did not want to take shortcuts. We would wait to get married until after I finished my IDF obligation—another nine months.

I also insisted on going to college. Ideally, I would finish military service, then graduate from college, then get married, and then (simultaneously) have kids and start a career. By marrying Zvi right after my IDF service, I would be changing the order of the equation's factors. I was willing to change the order, but I was not willing to skip college.

"You know it doesn't take a degree to have kids, right?" Zvi would joke when I pressed him to agree on this point. But he gladly accepted my terms, agreeing to postpone children until after I finished college. He just wanted to get married soon.

During the nine months of our engagement, Zvi frequently whisked me away on outings and to social gatherings. I loved the dinner parties with his friends, but he preferred getting out of the city and finding places where we could camp, bike, hike, or (his favorite) sail. Often, he would take me to a part of Israel that I had never seen. Israel is a small country, but much of it was unfamiliar to me. Zvi, on the other hand, seemed to have explored every inch of it. As we drove or hiked, he would share tidbits of information about the topography or history of each region. I marveled at the depth and breadth of his knowledge.

In these moments I could easily picture Zvi as a father. He did not possess Abba's tenderness, but he did possess a deep devotion to family and country. I knew that he would inspire our children to love their country the way he and I had. It warmed my heart to think of our children, the next generation of Israelis, one day planting their own lives into the land of their forefathers.

Our road trips and camping excursions allowed us to learn more about each other. I was struck by how different we were. I had been studious and diligent in school, and I learned by reading and studying. Zvi was immensely intelligent, but he learned primarily through life experiences. I had struggled with bodyweight insecurity throughout my teenage years, but Zvi had never cared about what others thought of him. He saw everything as either black or white, rational or idiotic, whereas I loved finding the nuances in every situation and argument. Over time, I realized that these differences—despite inciting a few arguments—were complementary and not contradictory.

Our military experiences also diverged. My training had been physically rigorous, but my service at IDF headquarters had never been dangerous. By contrast, Zvi had gone straight from training into combat. He had served in the Armored Corps and fought in the Six Day War. The war was a short but fierce conflict between Israel and the three enemy nations that shared its borders—Syria, Jordan, and Egypt. Zvi and his tank unit fought in the Sinai Peninsula, defending Israel's southern border against Egyptian troops.

It was strange to hear Zvi describe details of the conflict so vividly and personally. For me, the Six Day War was a blur of uncertainty and confusion.

At the time, I was only fourteen. All I knew was that our young nation had been attacked and that we were surrounded. Israel being small—a little larger than New Jersey—the fighting and bloodshed were unnervingly close all the time. During that week, my family and I hid with several other families in a neighbor's dark and damp basement. We huddled inside for what seemed like weeks, listening to the Israeli jets thunder overhead and waiting anxiously for radio updates. Such communications were limited, but usually encouraging. In the eighteen years since Israel's formation, the military had established itself as a strong, capable force—one not easily defeated. Despite the real danger, we all felt pride and exhilaration whenever we heard that Israel was successfully defending itself. We were no longer displaced and powerless. This was what our grandparents and great-grandparents had longed for, and what our parents had fought and labored to secure.

Waiting in that basement, of course, I had no idea that my future husband was on the front lines of that war, nor did I have any concept of the carnage around him. When it was over and Israel had won, my family and I came out of that basement with shouts of joy and a renewed sense of patriotism. For us, life quickly returned to normal. But for Zvi, life would never be the same. At age eighteen, he had witnessed the horrific realities of death and war. Half of his unit had been killed in the fight, many of whom were his closest friends. He was one of the fortunate survivors, but the terrible memories of that war would always remain, just like the shrapnel lodged in the back of his head.

Zvi rarely spoke about the war. Like my father, he almost never expressed grief or sought pity. I wished that I could be his confidante.

"What's the point?" he would ask when I pressed him. "I survived. I've moved on. A lot of other men didn't get that chance. It would be ungrateful of me to dwell in the past when so many were robbed of their futures."

Zvi's stoicism could be frustrating, but I also admired him for it. He was right. Many of his peers had suffered fates far worse than his own, and just one generation prior, millions of lives had been destroyed by a war that was far costlier than the one Zvi had fought in. We both had learned that evil, suffering, and death were real forces in the world, but they need not have the final word. We could pick ourselves up after hardship and press on with strength and resilience. We could build something beautiful and worthwhile.

This was the commitment that Zvi and I made to each other when we got married in 1972. The wedding, like every aspect of our relationship, happened in a blur. After the ceremony, Zvi whisked me off for a honeymoon in Tzfat, a village in the north of Israel. From there, it was back to Tel Aviv and the apartment we had rented as our first home.

The early days of life with Zvi felt chaotic. The apartment needed to be furnished and decorated, a task that we both took on with fervor, as a team. I contributed my sense of style and Zvi made some of our furniture, which, of course, spread sawdust throughout our home. There was always a mess to clean up, especially since Zvi did a lot of the cooking. I found myself longing for life to calm down, but for the first three years, the pace never slowed. This came as no surprise. Before marriage, I knew that Zvi would move us forward at breakneck speed. He was always working on the next project, planning the next trip, or pursuing the next career achievement. While I pursued a degree in textile engineering at the local college, Zvi kept our lives exciting.

As I brought my three-year degree to a close, we agreed to begin trying to have kids. As if on cue, I got pregnant and found out the baby was due around the time I would graduate. Sure enough, I earned my degree and the title of mother in the span of a few weeks.

Having a daughter in our lives felt miraculous and angelic. Zvi and I marveled that someone so tiny and beautiful could come from our two wild and chaotic lives. Receiving her into our arms felt like a tangible deposit of hope. Everything we had accomplished, everything we were building, was for her and any children who followed. She would grow up in Israel and enjoy the fruit of her parents' and grandparents' labors. And she, too, would play a part in building Israel's future. During those first weeks with her, I often thought about how my parents had once held me in their arms and dreamed of *my* future. I hoped I was doing those dreams justice.

Women of my mother's generation were typically content in the traditional roles of mother and housewife, but the women of my generation were steeped in Sabra lore. We felt an intense urgency to work alongside our male peers in professions designed to shape Israel's future. In addition to childrearing, we pursued educations and careers. The message ringing in our ears was, "You're a Sabra. You can do it all."

So, as soon as our daughter was old enough, I decided to enroll her in a daycare close to home. This freed me up to put my degree to use. By combining my formal education in textile engineering with my love for fashion, I felt confident that I could turn my part-time hobby of designing sweaters into a full-time business. Launching the startup in partnership with a friend, we purchased wholesale fabrics and carefully drew designs at home. Zvi's parents, who owned a small textile business themselves, generously allowed my friend and me to use their space to cut and sew our prototypes, which I then showed to the owners of local boutiques to see who might be interested in buying. The response was overwhelmingly positive. Our clothing was soon being sold in shops all over Israel. Eventually, we had to hire extra seamstresses to help with the sewing, which freed me up to focus on creating new designs.

While juggling family and business, I became pregnant a second time and gave birth to another daughter. With this beautiful little person also in our lives, it seemed as if I had it all—a handsome husband who was successful and adventurous, two angelic daughters, a profitable business, a good reputation, and a lovely home in the heart of Israel. When I considered all of this, I felt like echoing the words of King David, who said "the boundary lines have fallen for me in good places."

CHAPTER TEN

INTERRUPTION

"Hello, fine ladies! Where are you all off to?"

Zvi had just stepped inside our sunlit little apartment to find the girls sitting restlessly in their stroller while I darted around the house to tidy up. I pulled on a pair of high heels and snatched a tube of lipstick from the mantel. The girls and I were heading out to meet friends at a nearby café, and I was surprised that Zvi had come home so early.

Just as he said that he wanted to talk with me, one of our toddler daughters, whose hair had just been yanked by her sister, interrupted him with a dramatic wail. Whatever Zvi had wanted to talk about would have to wait. I was running late, and if I didn't get out the door soon, I knew that the girls would grow cranky.

Zvi sighed. "If I'd known you were going to be leaving in such a rush, I wouldn't have left the office early," he grumbled.

"I'm sorry," I told him as I maneuvered the stroller out the door. "We always go out at this time of day. Let's talk when I get back. Don't forget dinner is at your parents' house tonight."

With that, I waved goodbye and made my way down the sidewalk; the click of my heels sounding like a metronome. After a couple of blocks, I could see my friends and their colorful attire in the distance. Like me, they were young career women and mothers. Several afternoons each week, we would finish our work, pick up our little ones from daycare, and meet for an afternoon promenade on Tel Aviv's shaded streets. We were quite the sight. Our babies and toddlers were dressed to the nines. Older siblings wore dapper matching outfits and lounging infants sported bonnets that haloed their sleeping faces. Dressed to impress, we were the model Israeli women—gentle, compassionate, nursing mothers by night and bold, beautiful, businesswomen by day.

The responsibilities of motherhood did not preclude us from joining the work force. We did not work outside the home just to bring in extra cash. Ambitious and eager, we intended to leave a mark on the professional world. After wrapping up our workdays, we would pick up our kids and meet at outdoor cafés where we would sip cortados and bask in the late afternoon sunshine. We were a troupe of fashionistas with babes on our laps.

That afternoon, as I settled under the awning of our favorite café, I breathed in deep. The girls had fallen asleep during the walk over. A light breeze rejuvenated me after a long day of work. These afternoon get-togethers gave me a chance to enjoy a little peace of mind, something that was otherwise crowded out by busy schedules.

At age twenty-five, I looked for ways to maintain a perfect balance between work, home, marriage, and children. Like the experiments in my high school chemistry class, which taught us about maintaining a stable chemical reaction, I believed I could find the exact formula to keep everything balanced in my life. Sitting outside that café, I felt that I had attained a healthy equilibrium.

Once drinks had been finished and tabs settled, my friends and I set out toward our own homes. Facing us were dinners, bath times, and diaper changes. As I peeled away from the group and waved goodbye, I remembered that we were scheduled to eat dinner at Zvi's parents' house that night. There would be no mess to worry about tonight, at least.

As the girls and I approached the house, Zvi stepped outside and began locking up, jacket slung over his arm.

"Right on cue," he said. "I was just about to hitch up the horse and carriage to pick you up! Are you ladies ready for dinner?"

I smiled and nodded. Whatever exasperation I had caused Zvi in my hasty departure earlier that afternoon had dissipated. He was in a good mood. I loaded the girls into the car, climbed into the passenger seat beside him, and placed my hand on his arm.

"I'm sorry I had to leave in such a rush. What brought you home so early?" I asked.

Zvi didn't look at me, but I could tell that he was smiling.

"What? What is it? It's something good, isn't it?"

"I'll tell you when we get there."

The drive was short, but by the time we parked at his parents' house, I could hardly bear the suspense. Inside we progressed through the customary greetings, sat down at the dinner table, and blessed the meal together. As we passed the food, Zvi's father initiated the dinner conversation.

"So, son, anything new at work these days?"

I eyed Zvi. Rarely was there anything new to report at these weekly dinners, but that night I knew there was something important on my husband's mind.

"As a matter of fact, yes," Zvi replied. "I just found out about a possible trip coming up and was wondering if you and Eema might watch the girls so that Bracha and I could go."

"Both of us?" I asked before his parents could respond. "Why would I be going?"

Zvi loved taking me on work trips. Once, he had brought me along to Mexico City to explore a job offer. He had been enamored with the city, but I quickly made up my mind that I would never move there, mainly because I did not want our future children to grow up so far from Israel. An avid adventurer and man-of-the-world, Zvi was mystified by my mulish obstinacy. On the trip home, he told me that my decision was a "squandered opportunity." That evening, I could see the same excitement in him again.

"That's what I came home early to talk to you about. I was offered a job at Malden Mills in the US," he said. "They contacted me. They're opening a new department and they are looking for someone to run it. For now, they want us to come out and tour their facilities before I make a decision."

While his parents congratulated him, Zvi looked at me with boyish hope and excitement in his eyes. This was clearly a unique career opportunity for him. Malden Mills was one of the premier textile manufacturers in the United States, so for that company to pursue Zvi proved that he had established a strong reputation in the international textiles industry. This offer was far more prestigious than the position in Mexico City, and thus harder to turn down. Still, something in my heart sank.

"Wow, what a flattering offer!" I said, forcing a smile. "And you want to accept?"

"Well, I think we should at least take the trip over there," Zvi replied. "The company said they would put us in a nice hotel in Boston and let us explore the plant before drawing up any kind of contract."

"Sounds like a good deal to me," Zvi's father interjected.

"Yes, and we'd be happy to take care of the girls. It would be a nice break for the two of you," said his mother.

I knew they were right. It *was* a good opportunity, one that was at least worth considering. But I still felt cornered.

"We'll have to talk about it at home," I said. "But it's certainly a tempting offer!" I wanted to play the part of the supportive, game-for-anything wife.

Zvi turned to me again. He knew I was thinking about what had happened in Mexico City.

"Nothing is set in stone, Bracha. It would just be an exploratory trip," he said. "If it seems like a good fit, we can negotiate our time commitment. If the terms are not something you feel comfortable with, I'll turn it down."

I envied Zvi for his ability to be so carefree, so unburdened by worry or need for control, so firmly rooted in his identity. He would be the same person in Israel or anywhere else in the world. I wished I could possess his confidence.

Then one of my father's nature lessons came to mind. The strength of the sabra cactus, he had told me, was its ability to thrive in any soil. Although it could be found everywhere in Israel's streets and rural areas, it was not an indigenous plant in Israel; it had been imported from Mexico to Israel where it flourished in the desert soil.

Reflecting on my father's lesson, I realized that, as a Sabra, I should be tough enough to thrive anywhere. To be uprooted and successfully replanted might *prove* my Sabra-ness, not negate it. Maybe, I wondered, my life to that point had been a training ground for life in another part of the world. With these thoughts circulating in my mind, I told Zvi that we should go to Boston and explore the job opportunity.

After finalizing our travel arrangements, we kissed our girls goodbye and promised our parents that we would be back soon. During the long flight across the Atlantic, I thought about my childhood years in Ein Kerem, my simple roots, and all that my father had taught me about building a strong nation. Perhaps, I thought, an excellent short-term professional opportunity for Zvi and a family adventure in the US would help us make a better contribution in Israel.

The CEO of Malden Mills, the grandson of a Jewish immigrant to the US, gave us a "no holds barred" experience from the moment we landed in Boston—a nice hotel, free taxi rides, a tour of the textile mill and company headquarters. Enthusiastic about Zvi's professional capacity, he clearly loved the idea of helping us move to Boston. I could not deny that the position at Malden would be a step up for Zvi, and his job in Israel did not seem to offer him an opportunity for professional growth.

One evening near the end of our trip, while Zvi sat in a hotel room chair, he announced that he had to give the CEO a decision the next day.

"What do you think?" he asked me.

That night at dinner I had been weighing the pros and cons. I had realized that the only way to give Zvi a better professional future was to say yes. I had also come to see that a move far from Israel might cement us as a family. Boston was a beautiful city that supported a vibrant Jewish subculture. I could picture myself living there. The girls were too young to experience cross-cultural or social displacement. In fact, we would probably be able to return to Israel before they started elementary school. I also sensed that this move would be a catalyst for my own personal growth. Life was comfortable in Israel. I was content. But at age twenty-five, comfort was not my primary goal. I knew that we should accept the offer, but one thing still worried me.

"How long will we be expected to stay?" I asked.

"Well, initially he asked for three years . . ." Zvi began.

"Over my dead body!" I erupted. "*Three* years! Oh, no. We are not doing that."

"I know, calm down." Zvi was his typical, infuriatingly unemotional self.

"I will *not* . . ." I began. No amount of rationalizing would convince me to accept a three-year contract.

Zvi interrupted. "I know, Bracha. I knew you wouldn't agree to that. I told him as much. After some negotiating, he was willing to bring it down to a year. Do you think you could handle that?"

I was dumbfounded. "They'll still want you even if you'll only stay a year? And they'll pay for the move?"

"That's what he said."

A year was feasible. I hadn't expected anything less than a year and a half or two.

"Well?" Zvi asked, showing uncharacteristic patience.

I agreed with Zvi to move to the US. My response opened the door to a new future.

CHAPTER ELEVEN

YERIDA: LEAVING ISRAEL

B reaking the news to family and friends about our impending move was bittersweet. Zvi's parents and mine understood how important this opportunity was for his career. The experience he would gain at Malden would make him even more desirable to textile companies in Israel. My friends, too, were congratulatory. They expressed admiration for my willingness to move our young family in support of Zvi's career.

We had made it clear that our contract was only for a year, but many people expressed some resentment about our decision to leave Israel. Zionism had infused society at that time with a subtle contempt for anyone of Jewish heritage who chose the life of "exile."

The high value placed on immigrating to and remaining in Israel had originated from Zionists before the nation was established. These men and women had understood that an independent Jewish state would require strong will and a large population. Zionist missionaries went out to Jewish communities around the world, urging them to return to their ancient homeland and unite as one people. Many heeded their call, but it was not until World War II that diaspora Jews, facing existential threat, realized how fragmented and dispersed they had become. As a result, huge numbers of Jews began flooding into Palestine. This migration proved instrumental in the establishment of an independent Israel.

Israel passed the Law of Return in 1950. This law incentivized people to move to Israel by promising Israeli citizenship to any Jews or Jewish converts who decided to settle in Israel. Immigrating to Israel was often viewed as a spiritual act, an *aliyah*, which in Hebrew means "ascent." Like the Israelites of old, immigrants were seen as making their way up from the morass of life in diaspora into the glory of the Promised Land. Conversely, anyone emigrating from Israel to another country was seen as going "down," a movement from glory to the netherworld. This was called *yerida*, which is the Hebrew word for "descent." Those who left Israel were often viewed as highly suspect and treated with thinly veiled scorn.

As we prepared to move abroad, the call to immigrate to and remain in Israel was still forceful. At that time, the nation's border situation and economy were far from stable. Political and religious leaders communicated the need for more workers. Israeli couples were encouraged to adhere to the scriptural command to "be fruitful and multiply," but babies were more useful for ensuring the nation's *future* than for solving the immediate need for security and prosperity.

For these reasons, disparagement often emanated from friends and neighbors when Zvi and I announced our upcoming move, but I never experienced an outright rebuke, as might have occurred in the fifties and sixties. Since those decades, many people our age had "descended" to foreign universities and "ascended" again to apply their educations and skills in Israel. As a result, *yerida* still had a negative connotation, but it was more often used as a way to delicately shake one's finger at those who willfully chose to leave for selfish purposes rather than staying to work for the good of the nation.

I told myself that we were not being selfish, nor were we abandoning Israel. You could hardly call it yerida since what we had planned was more like an extended trip! Nevertheless, I still struggled with bouts of dismay. I worried about what others were thinking and saying about us, but more intense was the grief I felt in leaving my home and family. I was nervous about living in an unfamiliar place. I had never lived outside Israel. In fact, I had never been more than a few hours' drive from my family. It pained me to think of raising my girls so far away from their grandparents.

As our departure date approached, I increasingly realized how much I was about to forfeit. The routine but beautiful aspects of our lives—spontaneous trips to visit my parents in Ein Kerem, weekend hikes in the Judean hills, our weekly Shabbat dinner at Zvi's parents' house, speaking Hebrew at the market— would disappear in Boston.

I also began to worry about a long list of what-ifs. My parents were not yet old, but what if something were to happen to them while I was away? As their eldest child, I felt a deep responsibility for their wellbeing. Then, as soon as my fears about them subsided, I would find myself worrying about my girls. They would only be two and three when we arrived in Boston, but they would certainly be impacted by their new culture and surroundings, and I did not know how to navigate culture shock with two toddlers. I wondered if life in the US would change them so much that they might feel out of place upon our return to Israel. I wanted them to learn English, but I questioned whether that would make them deficient in Hebrew. Most grievous to me was the thought that their earliest memories of "home" might be in America, not Israel.

Zvi thought I worried too much. He never agonized over such things and saw no reason to entertain my concerns. His perspective, I knew, was right. We would only be living abroad for a year. It would be an adventure. Zvi's job prospects would look brighter, my mastery of English would be stronger, our girls would experience more of the world, and, most important of all, we would prove our Sabra resiliency. Our Israeli identities would not change. We would flourish in Boston and come back stronger than ever.

The day finally came for us to leave. Our belongings had been packed and shipped ahead of us; aside from the babes on our hips, our hands were free to embrace our parents at the airport. They kissed the girls, smoothing their hair. They commented sadly that our daughters would go through a lot of changes during our time apart, but we cheerfully encouraged them to visit anytime.

Despite my outward enthusiasm, saying goodbye to my father was heartrending. I had lived away from him for years, but saying goodbye that day felt different. In America I would not be able to stop by on weekends and the time difference would complicate our regular phone calls. I worried about him being left to mitigate my mother's bouts of depression alone.

Abba's clear blue eyes welled up with tears as he pulled me in close. I could feel his frame draw up straight as he tried to maintain composure.

"What will I do without my Bracha?" he whispered.

"I'll call lots, Abba. And I'll be back soon."

My mind filled with thoughts about how much my father had done for me over the years. I wanted to express my gratitude, but I was on the verge of tears and could not get the words out. Instead, I kissed him on the cheek, mustered a smile, and waved goodbye.

When we arrived in Boston, exhausted from the flight with small children, we waited for the shuttle that would take us to our new home. I immediately noticed the absence of palm trees and the significant drop in temperature. The sky was blue and cloudless like it had been when we left Israel, but the air was crisp, unlike anything I had experienced, even on Israel's coldest days.

"Zvi and Bracha?"

A man was waving at us from the curb. After a day of travel and navigating a sea of strangers, it was odd to hear our names. We waved and made our way over.

"Hello, I'm Daniel," the man said. "I work at Malden Mills. The boss asked me to pick your family up from the airport and take you to Andover."

I was grateful that Daniel would guide us to our new town. We loaded our suitcases in the trunk and set off, Zvi taking the passenger seat so that the two could talk. Zvi's English was much more fluent than mine, and I was too jet lagged to attempt anything beyond the basics. As we drove, I gazed out the window. It was autumn and the city was brimming with color. The bright reds and oranges of New England foliage were remarkable.

"So, you're the new guy everyone's been talking about!" Daniel said. "Coming in from Israel, right?"

"Yes," said Zvi. He was tired, too.

"And you got a place in Andover? That's surprising."

Despite my fatigue, my interest piqued. "Why is that?"

"I guess I would've expected you to pick a place in Brookline," he replied. "That's where folks like us tend to live."

"Folks like us?" I asked. "Are you from Israel, too?" I had not noticed an accent, but maybe he had been in the US for a while.

"No, no. I wish," Daniel said, meeting my eyes sheepishly in the rear-view mirror. "I've only visited. But my family is Jewish. A lot of Jewish families live in Brookline. We have a strong community, so I thought that you would be living there, being so far from home. But Andover is nice. It's just a little farther out of the way."

I felt a little disappointed. A robust Jewish community might make life in America seem more like home.

"I heard about Brookline," Zvi said. "But we're here to experience something new, not replicate the life we had back home."

Our rented apartment in Andover was simple, a brick, three-story complex with a pool. It seemed like a step down from our home in Tel Aviv. We bought bedroom furniture that we could ship back to Israel, but we placed garden furniture in the living room. Neither of us saw a reason to spend a lot of money on temporary housing.

However, Zvi did encourage me to invest my time in learning about the local culture and enabling myself to be self-sufficient. My English was not that good yet, and simple things like driving in a new city, speaking to a grocery clerk, and paying bills felt foreign and intimidating. I would have preferred to let Zvi do all that, but he knew I would need to build confidence and fend for myself. When I asked for help with a task, Zvi would stubbornly resist. "I'll be at the mill all day. You can do it. You're smarter than me. Figure it out!" Or he would say something like, "You can only get better if you practice. You will soon feel more comfortable here."

One early task was to find a daycare center for the girls. We wanted the girls to be immersed in English and enjoy time with other children. We also wanted to find a job for me. Zvi and I agreed that, given how little time we expected to stay in the States, a part-time job would help me to assimilate, practice English, and meet more people, all while earning some additional income. Thankfully, we found a daycare that would take the girls *and* hire me part-time, making it a perfect fit.

Life in America soon became ordinary and manageable. I quickly learned my way around the city and discovered that I had a better grasp of English than I thought. Although there were significant cultural differences, I had always been outgoing and most people were friendly and gracious. I found it easy to make friends. Once more I discovered that I could accomplish more than I had thought. Just as I had realized in IDF training, the "ceiling" of my self-imposed limits was not as low as I had been prone to believe. The more I accomplished each day, the more courage I found to try new things. I began to think about other ways to be productive. Then a thought occurred to me.

What if, when we returned home, we had one more child?

Zvi and I had always wanted to enlarge our family. Going through pregnancy in Boston would be an efficient and productive use of the time we had left. The trick would be to conceive at the right time so that my due date landed before our year in the US came to a close. I had "timed" my first daughter perfectly so that she arrived shortly after I graduated from college, but my second daughter had been a happy surprise. Could I time this baby to come before our year was up? I was willing to take the risk.

To my great satisfaction, it took us no time at all to get pregnant. He or she would be born just before our planned return to Israel. I could hardly believe my good fortune. Still in the early weeks of pregnancy, I only shared the joyous news with Zvi. I treasured the knowledge in my heart and carried it with me as I worked and took care of the girls.

While working at the daycare center, I decided to add one more job to my schedule—as a teacher of Hebrew at the local temple. I also began volunteering for Hadassah, the Women's Zionist Organization of America. As my network of friends and colleagues expanded, I discovered, to my surprise, that many people were interested in my Israeli citizenship. At fundraising dinners for Hadassah, for example, everyone wanted to hear about life in Israel, and no one there thought of our move to the US as a "descent." The American Jews I met spoke longingly of "the homeland," and some even hoped one day to make *aliyah* (to "ascend" to Israel by moving there), but few were cognizant of the discomfort I felt about my perceived yerida.

New experiences and challenges continued to come my way. I had never seen more than a few flakes of snow before moving to the US. Then came the winter storm of 1979. I was entirely unprepared for the record-breaking twenty-seven inches of snow that landed on the city that January. Zvi and I rushed home to take shelter with our girls as streets and storefronts shut down. We watched helplessly as the powerful winds blew snow drifts higher and higher. To my great relief, the Jewish community knew that we were not prepared to ride out the storm and rallied around us. Kind strangers and new friends showed up on our doorstep with hot food and other cold-weather necessities. However, the girls needed some better outdoor clothing, so I bundled up and ventured out to buy snowsuits.

After making the purchases, I trudged down the snowy sidewalks toward home with department store bags hanging from my wrists. The streets, usually so full of traffic, were completely empty. While I had been shopping, the power in one set of blocks had failed. Candles flickered inside dark apartment windows as people waited for electricity to be restored. Snow crunched beneath my feet. All of it was unlike anything I had ever experienced in Israel—a true adventure! I found satisfaction in the opportunity to brave the elements, to endure the cold and snow like a hardy New Englander—a pregnant one at that. I could not wait to share the story with family and friends back home around a Shabbat dinner.

As the months went by, I had become increasingly certain that the little life inside me was a boy. If I was right, Zvi and I woud give him a name that means joy: Ron.

CHAPTER TWELVE

RONNY

After nine long months of waiting, labor finally began. Zvi and I dropped our girls off with a babysitter, breathlessly promising them that we would be back soon with their new sibling. As we rushed through traffic toward Lawrence General Hospital, I held the handle above the passenger window and tried to relax before the next contraction. This being my third pregnancy, I was less nervous about labor and delivery than I had been with the first two. Every birth was different, I knew, but there was comfort in knowing that my body had survived this kind of pain before. Besides, the temporary suffering seemed like a small price to pay for the joy of welcoming a new little life into our family.

I continued to hope for a boy. Israeli culture places a high value on sons who can carry on the family name. I did not feel much urgency in this regard because I was still in my prime childbearing years, but I was eager to place a grandson in my parents' welcoming arms. I knew that a son would mean a great deal to Zvi, too. For him, our girls were perfect treasures to be cherished and championed. A son would be a potential protégé, someone with whom to roughhouse, teach woodworking and sailing, and take camping and fishing. I had fallen in love with Zvi, in part, because I had envisioned the kind of role model that he would be for his future sons.

Wishful thinking was not the only reason I felt sure this baby was a boy. There was also a deep intuition that I could not deny and that usually only mothers perceive. I had sensed it during the quiet nights when everyone was asleep, those hours when I most missed home. I had found comfort in visions of what life would be like when I returned to Israel with an olive-skinned, curly haired boy in my arms, and then watched him grow and awaken to the world, and heard him bubbling with questions that I could barely answer. I pictured his little feet walking in the dust and dirt of his homeland and imagined his scuffed knees as he scrambled up trees to eat fresh fruit. I pictured him growing up immersed in the wonders of Israel's cultural mosaic, and, one day, serving in the IDF just like Zvi and I had. I hoped that he would have Zvi's fearlessness, my curiosity, and my father's tenderness. But whoever he became, something told me that this little boy was going to be extraordinary.

The moment of our son's birth was only hours away. I could feel it. There was great pain to endure in the meantime, but soon everything in my formula for a good life would be aligned. We would be back home in Israel, Zvi would find amazing career opportunities, I would return to my beloved fashion design business, and our three beautiful children (with hopefully more to come) would live out their lives as second-generation Israelis. This vision carried me through the next several hours.

Finally, the moment came. With a final push, the baby was born. Zvi leaned in to kiss my head and I closed my eyes. Relief washed over me as my body relaxed into the knowledge that the worst of the pain was over. Soon I would be holding a new life in my arms.

Then I realized that an ominous silence had pervaded the room. No cheering nurses, no glad tidings from the obstetrician, and more importantly, no newborn cries. Everyone was either avoiding eye contact with me or gazing wordlessly at the baby in the obstetrician's hands.

"What? What is it?" I asked, panicked.

The doctor looked up and, misunderstanding my question, said, "It's a boy!"

My relief returned. For one terrifying instant, I had thought that I had somehow lost the baby. The doctor's tone, however feeble, assured me that no such catastrophe had taken place. Still, the baby was not crying and everyone was acting strangely.

I had to know what was happening. I struggled to sit up, holding my breath as the doctor checked the baby's airway. In that moment, I noticed how small he was. Something else was "off," too, but I couldn't get a good enough view to tell what it was.

"He's breathing," the doctor said, nodding to the nurses.

Zvi squeezed my hand as I collapsed back onto the pillows. Maybe everything was okay. The doctor snipped the umbilical cord and handed my baby off to a nurse for cleanup. I assumed that the nurse would then congratulate us and deposit Ron onto my chest for skin-to-skin bonding, but as Zvi and I watched, the doctor and his nurses transferred the small, still body to a nearby incubator. Panic surged again.

What is going on? Are they not going to let me hold him? Why is he so still?

Before I could voice my confusion, one of the nurses hurriedly rolled the incubator out of the hospital room with the obstetrician following close behind.

I wanted to scream.

At the doorway, the obstetrician briefly stopped and turned. "I'll be back shortly with your son's pediatrician." Then he was gone.

Confused, I looked to Zvi. His face was calm, but otherwise unreadable. I looked at the other two nurses buzzing about the room, but they continued to avoid eye contact with me. None of this was going the way it had when my daughters were born in Israel, and part of me wondered if these events were simply the American way of doing things. The thought reassured me. I tried to be patient.

To take my mind off the worry, I began to jabber to Zvi about being right to name him Ron, how we might share the joyous news with our families, how my mother would fret over my recovery, and how my father would be unable to conceal his joy. Zvi smiled and nodded, but I could tell his mind was elsewhere.

So was mine.

A doctor peeked in. "Mr. and Mrs. Horovitz?"

We nodded and waved him in.

"I'm Dr. Angelo," he said. He pulled up a stool beside my hospital bed. "I'm the pediatrician assigned to your son. I'm sure you're wondering where your baby is. I don't want you to worry. They're just doing some tests before they bring him back to you."

"Is something wrong?" Zvi asked, cutting right to the chase.

The doctor stopped fidgeting with his clipboard and looked at Zvi and me directly.

"Your son . . ." He paused for a second. "Your son is not going to be a football player."

Seeing our puzzlement, he added, "But maybe a poet."

I frowned. *Poet? Football player? What is he talking about?*

Dr. Angelo went on to gently explain that our son had been born underweight and with below-average muscle tone. He would need to be kept at the hospital while they ran more tests.

"When will I get to hold and nurse my baby?" I asked as Dr. Angelo stood up from his stool.

"I'm afraid that won't be possible for some time," he replied. "He is too small to be held and seems to have poor sucking reflexes. He'll need to be tube-fed for now. But I'll be sure to have the nurses bring him in so you can at least get a good look at him. I'm sorry, I know none of this is what you wanted to hear."

My eyes welled with tears. He was right. This was not the news I had hoped for. In a matter of minutes, everything had gone from stable to uncertain. Terrible words—malnourished, intubated, poor muscle tone—flew through my mind. I wanted to know why this had happened. I wanted to know when we could bring Ronny home, and I wanted to know when he would be ready for an overseas flight.

Just then, I looked up at Dr. Angelo's face. He looked tired. Something told me this was not the only difficult news he had delivered that day. He shook Zvi's hand, then looked at me with eyes full of compassion. "We're going to take good care of your son. Don't worry."

Soon, a nurse rolled Ronny's incubator back into the room, stopping just inside the door.

"Dr. Angelo has been in to see you?" she asked with hesitation in her voice.

"He has," Zvi said, striding across the room and drawing the incubator toward the bed so that I could see inside. We had both waited long enough.

"I want to make sure you know he's not ready to be held," she said.

Zvi nodded. I propped myself up to look at my son. Even after Dr. Angelo's visit, I was not prepared for what I saw. The baby behind the clear plastic was even smaller than I had remembered, and none of the miniscule movements of a sleeping newborn were perceptible. Covered with tubes and cords, he was as quiet and limp as he had been right after birth. The sight was unnerving. I held my breath as I waited to detect the slight rise and fall of his chest. It was there, but only faintly. Then I noticed his feet. They were turned inward at the ankles, the toes of each foot pointing crookedly toward each other.

I looked at Zvi. "Why . . ."

"Clubfeet," he said, meeting my gaze grimly.

Clubfeet! A birth defect? I thought. *This can't be happening.*

The list of Ronny's problems seemed to be growing longer by the minute. As I looked at the little boy in the incubator, so frail and vulnerable, the gravity of the situation sunk in. This helpless little child was my *son*. I was his *mother* and he needed me desperately. So far, his new world had only been filled with harsh lights and probing fingers. Strength, from where I knew not, arose in my heart.

"Hello, Ron," I said with a soothing tone. I could not hold him to my chest yet, but I could let him know I was near. "I'm your Eema. I'm here to take care of you."

I continued speaking to him, but Ronny showed no signs of response. His tiny ribcage just continued to rise and fall, rise and fall with each little breath.

After a while, a nurse returned to take Ronny back to the NICU. As Zvi and I watched them go, I wondered what Zvi was thinking. Aside from his matter-of-fact diagnosis of Ronny's feet, he had demonstrated almost no emotion.

"So, when should I pick up the girls?" he asked, confirming my suspicion that he was not fretting over Ronny.

I took a deep breath. Before the delivery, we had planned for Zvi to be with me for the birth and then to return home to watch the girls while the baby and I recuperated overnight. Now, with so many unknowns, I was less confident that I could stay at the hospital alone.

"Maybe the neighbors would keep the girls one more night so you could stay here with me?" I ventured.

Zvi frowned. "I don't think that's necessary. They're keeping Ronny in the NICU tonight, so you'll just be resting. I might as well get the girls and put them to sleep in their own beds. No need to disrupt their routines any further."

I nodded. As much as I wanted the comfort of having Zvi near, we had to think of the girls, too.

Zvi gathered his things, made sure no further developments were coming from Dr. Angelo or his staff, and left. He would manage affairs at home, putting the girls to bed and taking them to daycare in the morning before heading back to work.

"Call me if you find out anything new," he said as he kissed me goodbye. "And I know you aren't going to listen to me on this, but *don't worry*."

Zvi was right. That night, despite being exhausted, my sleep was fitful. It seemed like every time my mind started to calm down, the beeping and shuffling sounds of the hospital would wake me up and revive my anguished thoughts. The light of day brought little reprieve. The nurses had no answers for me, and they could not bring Ronny to me until the afternoon.

Just when I thought I could wait no longer, a nurse poked her head in the door. "Dr. Keller just paged us from the NICU, ma'am," she said with a smile. "He said he will be in to see you in just a moment."

"Dr. Keller? What about Dr. Angelo?"

"I'm afraid he's no longer with us," she said.

"What do you mean? He was just here yesterday!"

"I'm sorry, ma'am. I'm afraid he passed away. We got the call about an hour ago."

I could not believe the news. I had barely known him, but Dr. Angelo's calm and comforting demeanor the previous day had made him seem like a dear friend. I would later find out that he had died of a heart attack the day after Ronny was born.

"I'm very sorry to spring that kind of news on you," the nurse said. "But you'll be in good hands with Dr. Keller. He is an excellent doctor and should be able to answer all your questions."

Just then, a new doctor walked in.

"Mrs. Horovitz?" He was looking down at the paper on his clipboard.

"Yes, that's me."

"Your son. Does he have a name yet?" the doctor asked.

"His name is Ron."

He wrote the name down on his sheet. All my muscles were tense.

"Alright, Mrs. Horovitz. I'm Dr. Keller, the new pediatrician assigned to Ron. I received his test results early this morning and have been reviewing everything with other doctors. I just finished looking him over in the NICU and wanted to get you up to speed on what we know."

His demeanor and manner of speaking were quite unlike Dr. Angelo's. He reminded me of an IDF drill sergeant. Despite being in bed, I straightened my shoulders as if standing at attention.

"You have a problem," Dr. Keller said.

"What do you mean?"

"Your son Ron is physically and mentally disabled."

CHAPTER THIRTEEN

WHY NOT ME

Hearing those words felt like standing next to a bomb blast. My ears rang. My sight blurred. It took me a few seconds to realize that Dr. Keller was still speaking.

"Wait," I said, holding out my hand and motioning for him to slow down. I was confused. Up to that point, we had been under the impression that Ronny's problems were only physical. He was underweight and had clubfeet, but both could conceivably be corrected. Now Dr. Keller had said that Ronny was *mentally* disabled.

"We're not sure about the extent yet," he continued. "We'll have to run more tests. But whatever the cause, there's no question that he'll have many hurdles to overcome in order to . . ."

He cut himself short.

"In order to what?" I asked, afraid of what he might say. "What kind of . . . condition does he have?"

I could not yet bring myself to say the word *disability*.

"I told you," Dr. Keller said. "We're not sure."

"Yes, but you're his doctor," I pressed. "You know more than anyone about what's going on here. And I'm his mother, so I think I have the right to know. How severe do you *think* the problem is?"

"Like I said, we'll have to run more tests," he responded. "For now, the main thing is to help Ronny get stronger. He needs to gain weight and build muscle. Even that is going to be tricky since he can't breastfeed."

"That is not impossible," I said, hiding my fear.

"No, not impossible" he agreed. "But I'm telling you, Mrs. Horovitz, it's going to be extremely difficult. He's having a hard time keeping food down. The nurses are doing their best, but Ronny is going to require a lot of help to gain weight. I don't want you to be under any illusions. You should be prepared for the worst."

At that point, I had something like an out-of-body experience. I could barely comprehend what he was saying. I hoped that this nightmare would end, that I would wake up to everything being normal again.

I did not wake up. As soon Dr. Keller walked out of the room, I burst into tears. I realized that my neat, orderly world—the life that I had been working so hard to build—was falling apart. Now I was supposed to "prepare for the worst." Both the thought of losing my son and the thought of Ronny suffering long term were equally painful. Either way, I knew that life would be forever changed.

Humans have an almost universal tendency to want to know *why* bad things happen to them, to know the cause of suffering. I proved to be no different. In my hospital room alone, I began to wonder if Ronny's condition was random, or if I had done something wrong. I recalled that early in my pregnancy I had taken an aspirin. I wondered if Zvi had been exposed to dangerous chemicals at the mill. Maybe one of us had a genetic defect. Perhaps we could we have avoided the problem if we had known more about our families' medical histories, which had vanished in the war and Holocaust. One minute I was spiraling into worst-case-scenario thinking, and the next I was clawing for hope.

After I had cried and railed and agonized, I took a deep breath and reached for the phone to call Zvi. When he picked up, I could hear muffled voices and mill machinery in the background.

"Hello? Bracha? Is everything okay?"

I wasn't sure how to answer that.

"Have you spoken with the doctor?" he asked.

I looked out at the hallway and saw a nurse wheeling a woman toward the elevators. The woman was holding a swaddled newborn in her lap. Festive balloons tied to the wheelchair were floating peacefully above her. She was smiling at her baby, blissfully unaware of how easily the doctor could have come into *her* hospital room and delivered the worst news of her life.

That should be me, I thought. *I should be calling Zvi to tell him that Ronny and I are ready to be picked up, not . . .*

"Bracha? Do you need me to come?"

I realized that Zvi might interpret my long silence as news that Ronny had died.

"No, no. It's okay. You don't need to come." I proceeded to tell him about Dr. Keller's visit, trying to relay the information accurately without being overly pessimistic.

I waited for Zvi's reaction. There was a long silence. My eyes welled up with tears. *Is he disappointed? Angry? Does he feel as disoriented as I do?* A few more seconds passed. Just when I was about to prod him for a response, he spoke.

"Okay, so what's the plan?"

"The plan?"

"The doctor said we need to focus on getting Ronny's strength up, right? What's the plan?"

Zvi's voice exhibited no grief, no shock. I wondered if he had understood what I had just explained.

"How can you talk about a plan when you just found out that your entire life has been knocked off course?" I asked. I wished he would have expressed lament, at least for a moment. "Think of what this means for our family! Our plans for the future! Everything!"

Zvi remained silent, contemplating what to say next.

"I don't know about you," he said slowly and gently, "but I think this life is beautiful."

I had called Zvi expecting sympathy and comfort, but he had moved ahead, accepting what life had set before us. Without scolding me, he had presented me with a choice. In that overwhelming moment, I was not ready to make it.

To see Zvi quickly coming to a place of acceptance left me confused for a while. I wondered if his matter-of-fact response had been a manifestation of shock. I speculated that he might eventually come to his senses and comprehend the gravity of our situation. I also suspected that he might be hiding his weakness and pain with a strong façade, the way my father had covered over the pain of his Holocaust experiences. I also knew that he was not a man who endlessly wallowed in emotional pain.

After I hung up the phone, Zvi's words echoed in my mind. During the next hours and days, I gradually realized that I had been viewing life through a lens of *loss*—the potential loss of my son and the certain loss of normalcy. The pain of this realization propagated through my whole way of seeing the world. I had been building my life on the formula that I had learned as an overweight teenager—be a nice person, do the right thing, demonstrate discipline, and all would be well. Now I began to doubt all my simple formulas. Life, in fact, played tricks. It cheated. It could care less what I thought or deserved.

Then the truth hit me: Life might be a cruel cheat, but I still had a choice. Without saying as much, Zvi had made that choice clear. I had to decide what kind of person I would be in this situation. Would I be like my mother or my father?

Both had suffered. My mother had been displaced by war, ripped out of her home and country, and then deposited in a fledgling nation that promised a future for her children but almost nothing for her. Her chosen response was to succumb to self-pity, to live as a victim. She had cast a sad pall over our home.

My father had a number tattooed on his wrist. He went through a Nazi death camp. He lost his entire family. Yet he chose to believe that beauty transcended life's ugliness. As I was growing up, his response to severe hardship was like a ray of sunlight beaming through dark clouds.

I knew that I, too, had to make a choice.

Knowing the right thing to do is not the same as being able to authentically *experience* it. I sincerely wanted to respond like my father and Zvi, but I struggled to find the strength. How could I say life was beautiful when it had dealt Ronny such a blow? Instead of bringing a healthy baby boy home from the hospital and joyously introducing him to his sisters, I was visiting him in the neonatal intensive care unit and weeping at the sight of his deformed, malnourished little body hooked up to tubes.

This? Beautiful?

It was not beautiful. What I had *before* was beautiful. I had a picture-perfect family, an international adventure, a schedule undisturbed by inconveniences, and a forthcoming happy return to Israel. Just two days earlier, my life had resembled a lovely painting set in a gilded frame. Now, as horrible as it felt to admit, I felt that Ronny's arrival had introduced a random splatter on the canvas, one that had marred everything. I felt guilty about it, but I sometimes wished that he had never entered the picture.

Why me? I kept asking myself.

Sometime in the blur of those days, as my soul raged and rebelled, a pivotal thought came to mind.

Why not *me?*

I remembered the horrible Holocaust and war stories told by my parents and neighbors. I had overheard strangers on the bus who recklessly discussed the atrocities they had witnessed. My blood had boiled as my teachers wrote out the grim realities of history on their chalkboards. I had grown up in a community marked by war, genocide, poverty, famine, and disease. That being the case, why did I expect to be exempt from hardship? In a world where horrific things happened to good people, why *not* me?

The thought was sobering. All my life, I had looked up to my father. He had shown me what it looked like to stand up after severe hardships. And yet, I had foolishly assumed that I could attain his strength and courage without being struck down myself. Now, after receiving news that felt like a mortar explosion, I realized that choosing to be resilient and joyful in the face of suffering would take more than I could imagine.

Thoughts like this gave me moments of resolve, but there was plenty of wavering during the ensuing days and nights. Postpartum hormones likely played a significant role in these ups and downs, but as test after test came back with discouraging news about Ronny, it was impossible not to feel overwhelmed and discouraged. In addition to being underweight and clubfooted, the tests showed that Ronny had misaligned hips and such poor muscle tone that he could not move any of his limbs. The doctors also found evidence of severe neurological problems.

As the days in the hospital drew on, the doctors said that Ronny's chances of survival had improved. This good news shifted the focus of my worries toward the long-term hardship that Ronny and our family would face. That reality grew bleaker when the doctors informed us that our little boy would never walk, talk, or even hear. And then one morning Dr. Keller dropped another bomb.

"I think, if we are strategic, we can give him a decent quality of life. He should make it about a year. I wouldn't give him more than twelve months, though."

By this point, I had begun to develop a bond with Ronny. I had only been allowed a few hours with him each day, but as I held him, my maternal instincts had begun to awaken. Whole and healthy or not, this little boy was my son and he needed me. When Dr. Keller disclosed his prognosis, I felt my maternal instincts roar to life.

Why only twelve months? I thought. If Ronny had defied the odds by surviving this long, then he could surprise everyone by living much longer than a year. I knew that Dr. Keller's statement was merely conjecture. The doctors had not yet landed on a precise diagnosis, so there was no way for him to confidently estimate Ronny's life expectancy. I felt certain that we could offer our son much more than one year.

"But just a few days ago you also told me to prepare for the worst," I countered. "You led me to believe Ronny wasn't likely to live more than a couple days."

"That's true. By all accounts he shouldn't have . . ." Dr. Keller began.

I did not want to hear it. I had confidence that he could outlive the doctors' grim expectations.

"So you *could* be wrong about this too, right?" I asked.

"Well . . ."

I wasn't about to let up. "I mean, from what I can tell, nobody knows what's wrong with Ronny. So, technically, who's to say he couldn't turn out completely normal?"

I knew this was likely an overstatement, but I also knew that Dr. Keller had no basis to say that Ronny would only live a year when almost all of his information was speculative. There was still a *chance* that Ronny might walk or talk someday. We could at least hope.

I was beginning to see new dimensions to the reality of suffering. If Ronny's future—the length and quality of his life—was going to depend on someone, then why not me? I was his mother, the one who had nurtured his life within my body, the one with whom he shared the deepest bond. I began to develop a new vision for life. By sheer determination and love, I could help my son rise above his limitations. I still had moments of doubt, frustration, and grief, but I decided to never give up on Ronny. Maybe I could salvage my picture-perfect life. Why *not* me?

CHAPTER FOURTEEN

WALLS

Over the next several weeks, I spent as much time with Ronny as the hospital would allow. It was difficult to be away from Zvi and the girls, but I knew that I had to take care of our family's weakest link. And weak he was.

The primary focus was to help Ronny gain weight and develop strength. He couldn't nurse and, even with a feeding tube, experienced frequent reflux due to his feeble esophageal muscles. Every ounce of milk that Ronny could keep down mattered. He required an all-consuming amount of care.

Our faithful efforts began to pay off. Like the tenuous first days of spring, Ronny slowly but steadily gained weight. He started to look and feel less skeletal. As his muscles strengthened, he developed the sucking reflex that allowed him to drink milk from a bottle. Every victory for Ronny served as a reminder for me to not give up. I could see that this little boy wanted to live.

The doctors and nurses marveled at Ronny's fighting spirit. They began to speak of sending him home, a development that filled me with both joy and trepidation. I was thrilled that Ronny might be well enough to leave the hospital, but I was nervous about how to integrate him into our family's routine. I was not sure that home could ever be normal again. I worried about the girls' reactions, about the neighbors' curious looks, and about when we could return to Israel.

At that point, Zvi was the only one among family members and friends who knew about the severity of Ronny's issues. He had supported me practically by caring for the girls and by continuing to provide financially. I was grateful for his steadiness, but I wished he could have been more emotionally sympathetic. Zvi didn't like to dwell on the unknowns, so I never felt like I could be completely transparent about my concerns.

"It is what it is," Zvi would say. "What's the point of looking back or getting ahead of ourselves? We'll manage."

Zvi's struggle to reveal his emotions was not the only reason I sometimes felt isolated. Unlike when my daughters were born, no visitors came to see Ronny and me in the hospital. Our relatives and closest friends were in Israel. Not that I wanted visitors. I did not want people to feel sorry for us or ask questions that I was not prepared to answer. The situation was too raw and personal. Nevertheless, I was alone.

A few days after Ronny's birth, I did inform my parents, but I kept the information vague. Ronny's chances of survival at that time had looked grim, and I did not want to burden them until we knew more.

"You have a grandson!" I told them with forced, artificial excitement.

In the shower of congratulations and questions that followed, I struggled to hold back my tears and keep my voice from cracking. Hearing my father's voice was even more difficult than I had expected. I had dreamed of proudly and joyfully announcing the arrival of his first grandson. However, I felt weighed down by *shame,* and the fact that I felt ashamed of my son made me ashamed of myself.

My parents were naturally curious about why Ronny and I were still in the hospital, but wanting to shield them from the truth, I simply said that Ronny was "a little weak." I then evaded questions that would force me to divulge the unsightly details of Ronny's situation and wrapped up the phone call as quickly as I could. I saw no reason to make them sad. They were far away. They could do nothing to help.

After I hung up the phone, I felt lonelier than ever. In choosing to protect my parents from the harsh news, I had closed off another door to share my sadness, disappointment, and angst. There was no one with whom to share my burden. I told myself this was the way it had to be. With examples like Zvi and my father ever before me, to be anything other than tough seemed un-Israeli.

I also despised the thought of being an object of pity. A pitiable life was antithetical to my follow-the-formula approach to life, to being a Sabra woman with a perfect, adventurous, and upwardly mobile family. *That* was the image I wanted to project of myself and my family. And staying in the hospital—safe from peering eyes—made it easier to maintain the veneer of perfection. At home the facade would become exponentially more difficult to sustain. Friends, neighbors, and coworkers would easily see through my standard deflection: "He's doing well. He's just a little weak." People would want to hold him. They would encounter his limp, malformed body and know that something was terribly wrong, at which point they would spout endless expressions of pity. Every interaction involving Ronny would be awkward, and when people would say goodbye they would whisper to each other, "Poor Bracha." I could foresee it all.

Inevitably, the time came for me to face these fears. Ronny had been in the hospital for about a month, and while his situation was still precarious, the doctors believed that he would progress best if nurtured at home.

As I walked out of the hospital with Ronny that day, everything felt surreal. As long as Ronny had been held in the hospital, there had been a degree of separation between his world and mine. Now the full integration would begin— in our leaf-strewn neighborhood, in the rooms of our home, with my daughters, and in the mundane intricacies of daily life. It felt daunting.

I reminded myself that my daughters had also seemed new and unfamiliar, once. They had each dramatically changed our family's dynamic. Each in her own way, they had made our family more complete. It eased my mind to think of this. I had to trust that Ronny would also integrate into the family's fabric. He would, of course, present us with significant challenges, but I hoped that the picture of our family could still be beautiful.

Over the next couple of months, without help from nurses, I worked tirelessly to care for Ronny's needs and transported him to weekly doctor appointments. Due to his frequent reflux, it became a full-time job to keep him fed and in clean clothes. He gradually gained weight and muscle tone, but Ronny could not independently move his head or limbs. Doctors told me this would always be the case, but I spent hours each day moving Ronny's arms and legs for him, hoping that his muscles would eventually get stronger. I would also talk, clap, and wave toys in front of his eyes looking for signs of awareness. If Ronny had a chance to improve, I could not give up.

In Ronny's fourth month of life, it was time for a routine physical exam. Ronny had been increasingly able to track motion with his eyes, and he would occasionally make little cooing or gurgling noises like his sisters had at that age. So, I hoped the doctor would give me good news about Ronny's development. But I also knew that most four-month-old babies were beginning to roll over independently, push themselves up with their arms, and lift their heads. Ronny had not come close to reaching *any* of these developmental markers. As I drove Ronny to the appointment, my stomach was in knots. I was terrified of what the doctor might say. Perhaps Ronny would surprise us and move his head a little during the appointment. I was determined to be optimistic.

After a brief wait, the doctor called us into his examination room. He laid Ronny on the exam table.

"Alright, little guy," he said. "Let's take a look at you."

"He looks stronger, doesn't he?" I asked hopefully.

Nothing about Ronny's limp, scrawny body suggested the word "strong," but because the doctor had seen him at his worst, he kindly did his best to agree.

"You know," he said, "I can tell he has gained some weight. I'm just going to take some measurements to see how how he's doing on the growth chart. While I do that, why don't you answer a few questions for me. How has Ronny been doing? Has he hit any of the milestones we talked about at his last appointment?"

"Oh, he's doing *great*," I said. "I can't believe how much he's improved!"

By projecting optimism, I hoped I might deter the doctor from focusing on Ronny's problems.

"Is Ronny following you with his eyes? Is he smiling yet? Giggling?" he asked.

The doctor placed his hand on Ronny's neck and gave it a small tickle. Ronny neither giggled nor squirmed.

"Yes, his smiles are *so* cute. I really hope you get to see one today," I said truthfully. I did not mention that Ronny had not displayed any normal signs of alertness or attentiveness. In fact, I was still unsure whether he could hear. Whenever I had clapped my hands loudly to test his hearing, Ronny had never reacted. But on that day, I was not about to suggest anything pessimistic to the doctor. I only wanted good news.

The doctor looked up from his notes with an expression of lament and told me that Ronny had not reached any of the normal physical, emotional, or relational markers.

"He *has* grown a little since last time," he said. "But . . ."

"That's great news!" I interrupted. "So, what do we need to be working on next? I really think Ronny is ready for more stimulation. I can tell he's slowly gaining muscle by doing the exercises I have been doing with him. Maybe we could get him into specialized physical therapy."

The doctor looked reticent.

"Well, we can talk about that," he said. "But let's not get ahead of ourselves. First things first. Is Ronny exhibiting *any* independent movements yet? Have you seen him turn his head? Lift his arms or legs? Anything of that nature?"

While I wavered, trying to think of a way to put a spin on the disheartening truth, the doctor pressed a stethoscope to Ronny's chest and back, listening to his heartbeat and lungs.

"Well, it's hard to say." I said with a forced smile. "There *have* been a couple times when I laid him down and came back to find his head facing the opposite direction."

As the exam proceeded, I kept willing Ronny to make a small, independent movement of some kind. I knew that the four-month checkup always ended with the pull-to-sit test, and I desperately wanted Ronny to pass. So, when the doctor gently lifted Ronny's arms in an attempt to bring him from a supine to a sitting position, I held my breath and watched.

Ronny did not have the strength to participate in the action. Instead of lifting his head and engaging his core as most babies do, Ronny's head lay limply on the table. My heart sank.

The doctor sighed and let Ronny's arms down gently. Turning to me with a grave look on his face, he said, "Mrs. Horovitz, I'm afraid Ronny's case is quite serious."

"What do you mean by serious?" I asked.

"I'm sorry, but I mean that your son is severely disabled. I think you need to come to terms with the fact that he isn't going to progress like a normal baby."

I tried to interrupt him, but he didn't stop.

"I know this is difficult for you," he continued. "And we can put him in physical therapy. But even then, I need you to understand that Ronny will *never* be able to sit up or crawl."

I was not about to accept such a verdict without a fight.

"I understand that Ronny faces some challenges!" I said defiantly. "But look at him! He has grown so much in such a short amount of time! He's more alert and he's smiling and he's starting to track movements and . . . and I just know he is going to prove you wrong!"

The doctor looked down at Ronny. The medical reality did not align with my words. After a moment, he sighed and looked back at me. "I don't know. You seem like you could go through walls."

I had not expected that response, but it felt good to hear. That was exactly how I felt! During the previous four months, I had felt trapped in a room of limitations and impossibilities. Invisible walls surrounded me and there seemed to be no door, no windows, no way out. Doctors and nurses just kept telling me that I was trapped, that this room was my new normal, and that I needed to accept it.

But I had seen supposedly impossible things happen before. I believed I could go through walls.

CHAPTER FIFTEEN

FEAR OF VULNERABILITY

My visions of "going through walls" soon proved misleading. I had envisioned surgeries magically erasing Ronny's physical problems. I had hoped for miraculous therapies that would allow Ronny to grow and develop normally. But as the days and weeks repetitiously crawled along, and as Ronny and I cycled through a parade of doctors, I made more and more concessions to medical reality. The word "severe" had not been used flippantly. Despite proving himself to be a fighter, Ronny's health never transitioned beyond the classification of "vulnerable."

My days never transcended the stage of "trying to keep Ronny alive." Of course, all parents of newborns experience this frightening, heavy responsibility. Having already had two babies, I understood how tiring it is to be a parent. But it was far more demanding to take care of Ronny than my daughters. There were real, day-to-day dangers that threatened his survival. Most days, the task of keeping Ronny alive required all my energy. I remained trapped within the walls of those demands.

In a closed, hermetically sealed space, oxygen depletion leads to exhaustion. The same can happen to the human soul when a person is locked in, unable to see a horizon, and facing endless burdens without hope. This was happening to me. Fortunately, Zvi saw me turning blue.

"You're taking on too much," Zvi said one day when my spirits were especially low. "Why don't you back off a little? Ronny is doing well. You don't have to run yourself ragged."

I shook my head. His words expressed sincere concern for my wellbeing, but he did not understand that I *could not* relax. In the worst-case scenario, "backing off" might mean that Ronny could slip toward death. More immediately, I might miss an opportunity to help Ronny make a breakthrough, and that thought was unbearable. I longed for Israel, and we could not go back until Ronny had improved and our lives were back in order. So, to focus on myself rather than on Ronny's progress would only prolong our return home. When Ronny was better and we were back in Israel, *then* I could relax.

When Zvi realized that I would not reduce my care for Ronny, he decided to reconnect us with the world outside the walls. He talked about taking family walks in our neighborhood and having friends over for dinner. He suggested that we return to the synagogue on weekends. In these ways, we could pump some oxygen into the room without neglecting Ronny.

I wanted to say yes, but the prospect of re-entering public life made me feel like I had during the Six Day War. Surrounded by threats from the outside, it seemed like a time to take shelter, not a time to be exposed. I did not want Ronny to be a spectacle. Surgery had taken care of his clubfeet, but he was still scrawny and awkward looking. On top of that, his constant drooling and spitting up meant that I had to frequently wipe his chin and change his clothes when we were out. Underlying my protective maneuvers was the fear of exposing my imperfect life, of being "that mom with the disabled boy."

Whenever I shared these insecurities with Zvi, he would respond by saying, "People aren't going to pity us unless we are acting pitifully." He did not care what people thought but gave them the benefit of the doubt, nonetheless. Most people, he assured me, would *admire* us for our efforts to love and care for Ronny.

Over time, I came to realize that it was unrealistic to focus all my efforts on "going through walls." I had to learn to bring fresh air into my world. Otherwise, I might not have the strength to care for Ronny and our daughters. I could not escape our new reality, but I could learn how to make it sustainable.

We began to make forays out of the house and into the broader world. To maintain some semblance of "the perfect family" in public, I always made sure that everyone was impeccably dressed. Wearing nice clothes had successfully improved my mood and confidence ever since that day when, as a teenager, I had stepped into the little dress shop. Now I hoped that fine attire would detract attention from Ronny. I hoped that people would look at me and the girls rather than ask to see the baby in the stroller. Even if they did ask, they would find Ronny decked out in dapper clothes, his oddly shaped ears strategically covered with a hat or bonnet. Clothing, I hoped, would give me some power over his imperfections.

In addition to getting us out of the house more often, Zvi also thought it would be helpful to invite people to our house. One such occasion, when Ronny was about seven months old, had a dramatic impact on my long-term outlook.

Zvi had suggested we invite a friend from work, Robert, and his family over for dinner. I initially resisted the idea. I already felt overwhelmed and hosting a dinner party for strangers sounded exhausting. I encouraged Zvi and Robert go out for drinks instead, but eventually Zvi convinced me. Robert and his wife Kathleen were nice and easygoing, he said. They were new to the area and had a daughter who was about the same age as our girls. The kids could play, the adults could talk about our shared experience of moving to a new city, and we could ease back into the habit of entertaining people—something we had missed doing ever since moving to America.

On the day of the dinner party, I spent hours prepping the meal, getting the house ready, and picking out clothing for the family to wear. I felt anxious about what these strangers might think when they met Ronny, but I had already come up with a plan to minimize their interaction with him. After a brief introduction, I would set Ronny on a blanket in the living room and give everyone a tour of the house. Then, while the four of us mingled over appetizers and ate our meal, I would be free to pop in and out of the living room to check on Ronny. Maybe our guests would be oblivious.

When the doorbell rang, I was sitting on the floor with Ronny, exercising his arms and legs. I got up and nervously glanced at Zvi. He smiled reassuringly and opened the front door. Standing on our New England doorstep was a beautiful family of four. Neatly dressed and bespectacled, Robert and Kathleen possessed a warm, college-sweethearts attractiveness. They smiled broadly. Holding out a bottle of wine, Robert began introducing himself and his family. He jokingly warned our girls to beware of his daughter's outgoing spirit, which made them giggle. All the while, my eyes were locked on the little boy in Kathleen's arms. He wasn't the toddler I had expected, but a baby about the same age as Ronny. My heart sank.

The baby let out a happy squeal and pumped his arms and legs, almost knocking Kathleen off balance.

"I heard that you just had a baby, too?" Kathleen queried as everyone stepped inside.

"Yes, Ronny! He's over there in the living room, just getting some time on his mat," I replied. I hoped that my enthusiasm would mask the uneasiness I felt. Ronny, I knew, had not moved from where I had left him on the floor. Kathleen's son, meanwhile, was bobbing up and down on her hip, smiling at me with huge, dimpled cheeks. The contrast was almost too much to bear.

"Oh, perfect!" she said. "Bobby loves playing on the floor! And it's a good thing, since he's getting so hard for me to handle! Do you mind?" She gestured with her head toward the living room.

I led the way. I wanted to get to Ronny first, just in case there was anything I could do to make the juxtaposition between him and Bobby less awkward. It was a pointless endeavor. Wiping away a little drool and rearranging Ronny's hat to better cover his ears could not hide the truth.

Robert and Kathleen responded graciously; they recognized that something was wrong, but they did not gush with phony sympathy. Their kindness helped to set me at ease, and soon our conversation was flowing naturally.

After Zvi handed them drinks, Robert and Kathleen mentioned that they were looking to buy a house in our neighborhood, to which Zvi responded by suggesting we all take a walk around the block. They liked the idea, but they questioned what to do with the babies on the floor.

"You all go ahead," I said. "I can keep an eye on the boys."

Once everyone else had departed, I looked at my son next to Bobby and wondered how the two could be so close in age. Growth charts and development milestones had been rather abstract for me, but seeing them side by side highlighted just how far behind the curve Ronny was. Being in the room with Bobby, plump and animated, made Ronny's situation seem even more daunting.

Love and sorrow for Ronny welled up inside me again. I wondered if this shocking contrast was what people would always see when they looked at him. It grieved me to think that they would be so fixated on his physical problems that they would fail to see him as a person. I wanted friends to see what I saw: his humanity and his fighting spirit. When I looked into his sweet, clear blue eyes, I knew that Ronny was stronger than he looked. I believed that Ronny could live longer than everyone expected—perhaps even into adulthood. Then I realized that I needed to take better care of myself. I would need mental and physical strength. For years it had bothered me that I had not maintained the level of fitness I had achieved in IDF training. Having lost so much ground, I could see no way to make changes.

I thought of Kathleen holding Bobby, the way she struggled to manage him when he was in her arms. Soon, Bobby would be walking, and Kathleen's tired arms and back would get a break from the strain. I, on the other hand . . .

It became clear that I could not afford to keep running my body and emotions into the ground. If I wanted Ronny to live a long and happy life, I needed to practice endurance instead of settling for exhaustion—for my sake *and his.*

Sitting on the floor with the two boys, a proverb that my father had often quoted resurfaced in my mind.

If I am not for myself, who will be for me?

But if I am only for myself, what am I?

If not now, when?

When my father first shared the proverb with me, I asked him what it meant. His answer was thoughtful and instructive.

"Well, it prompts you to ask yourself three questions," he explained. "The first bit, the 'If I am not for myself' part, is asking you to consider how much you value yourself."

He paused upon seeing my perplexed expression.

"I know what you're thinking," he continued. "We've always taught you to put others before yourself. But think about it this way: If you don't value your things, they get broken or lost and no longer serve their purpose, right? It's the same when you don't value yourself. While you think that you're doing something noble, you're just growing weaker until you can't serve your purpose."

"What *is* my purpose?" I asked sincerely.

"That's what the second part is about," he said. "It asks you to think about *what* you are if you are *only* for yourself. If your only purpose is to serve yourself and ignore other people, then you go from a who to a what. It means that your purpose is to serve others."

Abba paused and looked away, as if he was remembering something or someone in the past. After a couple of seconds, he looked back at me.

"And the last part?" he said with a smile. "'If not now, when?' *That* is encouraging you to stop making excuses and start right away."

The sound of Zvi and our guests at the front door broke my reverie. They entered, praising the smells of dinner that wafted through the house. With both boys content on the floor, I jumped up and began to set the table. The proverb and its meaning lingered in my thoughts. I wondered what "to be for myself" might look like.

I could hear Zvi laughing at an animated story that Robert was telling about his first fitness class at the YMCA.

"He signed up for a membership that same day," said Kathleen. "I never expected it to last, but he's been going consistently for months. He even has me going with him now!"

Captivated by what I had heard, I stopped placing napkins and entered the living room.

"That's one reason why we're looking for a house in this neighborhood," Robert continued. "We noticed that there's a nice Y just down the road from here, and we like that there are so many families and parks in the area. And now that we know you live here, too . . ."

"The YMCA?" I asked, butting in.

"Yeah!" Robert said. "Do you and Zvi have a membership?"

"No, but I want to go," I said with a tone of urgency.

If not now, when? I thought.

Zvi looked at me in surprise. I had not expressed open interest in exercise since leaving the military eight years earlier.

"You should!" Kathleen said with a smile. "The classes are excellent, and it has been good for me to get out of the house and do a little something for myself, you know?"

I did not know. I had forgotten to be "for myself." But now I could see that I needed to take care of myself to better take care of my family.

CHAPTER SIXTEEN

THE SCRIPT

Before I joined our neighborhood YMCA, my exercise experience had consisted entirely of the three intense months of IDF training. Since then, I had failed to practice the lessons I had learned in the military about physical discipline. I was twenty pounds overweight, perpetually exhausted, and always on the brink of anxiety and depression.

Fortunately, the YMCA offered many classes for beginners like me. I joined two in hopes that they would force my workouts to be consistent and demanding even when my motivation waned. Soon, I was going to the gym almost every day. After a few weeks, my motivation increased, perhaps due to the endorphins released during workouts. I noticed positive changes in my health. The gym membership got me out of the house and engaging with others, which scratched my extrovert itch. It gave me access to classes about nutrition and exercise that satisfied my love of learning. It taught me about the mind-body connection, which empowered me to spend less time on irrational worries about Ronny. Perhaps greatest of all, it gave me a clear and realistic obstacle to overcome. After months of pushing on Ronny's intangible walls (often without seeing results), it felt good to set a tangible goal, work at it, and achieve success. Exercise soon became a grounding element of my life, the one realm where life followed a rational formula. It gave me hope that, while Ronny's problems may have taken me on a detour, it was possible to get my life back on the desired trajectory.

The terminus of that trajectory was still Israel. Due to Ronny's condition, Zvi and I had postponed our return to Israel and arranged to stay longer in

Boston. Zvi's company was glad to keep him on board, the girls were doing well, and Ronny was getting the care he needed, but everything inside me longed for home. I missed the pastoral charm of Ein Kerem, the burgeoning energy of Jerusalem, the multicultural clamor of Tel Aviv, the comforting sound of Hebrew, the mouthwatering smells of Mediterranean food—the secure feeling of *home*.

Most of all, I missed our friends and family. The move to America had isolated us more than we had anticipated. We had friendships, but they were superficial compared to those we had left behind. Not expecting to stay in Boston for more than a year, we had sometimes held our American friends at an emotional arm's length in hopes of avoiding painful goodbyes. For many expatriates, these types of choices are common. In our case, due to Ronny, we experienced deep grief that was best managed alone.

That is why, even two years after Ronny's birth, I continued to shield my parents from the extent of his issues or my heartbreak. By that time, he was doing far better than his doctors had forecasted. The treatments and therapies I had lobbied for had been more successful than even I had dared to hope. Ronny was gaining weight, building strength, and even learning to sit upright with minimal assistance. Due to these signs of progress, I believed that a breakthrough was just around the corner and therefore saw no point in sharing only bad news with my parents.

I judiciously shared whatever encouraging tidbits I could with my parents. They knew Ronny was "slow," but they did not know the magnitude of his developmental delays. I assured my parents (and myself) that Ronny was improving rapidly and that we would be headed home in no time.

Perhaps my parents sensed that I was concealing the full story from them, or maybe they were simply impatient to see their grandkids, but after two years of being held at bay, they announced that they were coming to Boston for a visit. My longing to see them was woefully overshadowed by nerves. As much as I hated to admit it, I preferred for them to stay in Israel where I could feed them the truth in manageable portions. I had also hoped that I might buy enough time for Ronny to improve, so that my parents would never have to know how grim things had been at the beginning.

In a last-ditch effort to dissuade them from coming, I (baselessly) said that we would be returning to Israel soon. But they were adamant. They had decided to come and had planned to stay for a month.

Left with no alternative, I realized that I needed to change my approach to sharing information with my parents. On the phone and in letters, I began revealing more. I did not want reality to shock them. Still, I made no mention of "disability."

On the day my parents arrived, our daughters' squirrelly anticipation melted into shyness. Clinging to my legs in the airport, they smiled furtively as their grandparents showered them with flattery and affection. While they played hard to get, Zvi and I went through the motions of greeting our long-awaited guests. That's how it felt to me—going through the motions—because amidst the joy of our reunion there lurked a silent anguish. I felt tense and watchful. As we kissed cheeks and inquired after everyone back home, I fought an urge to stand between my parents and Ronny. My deepest concern was that Ronny's physical problems would prevent them from seeing his true personality. I was afraid that my parents would look at him and be unable to see past the two greatest Israeli sins: weakness and passivity. I wanted them to see that life had dealt him a terrible hand, but that he had not folded. To the contrary, he had overcome the doctors' predictions of early death or living in a vegetative state.

Ronny had become capable of independent movements. Although he was nonverbal, his big blue eyes spoke volumes about his soul. It just took patience and determination to see his qualities. With my parents now standing on the threshold between "not knowing" and "knowing," I was anxious to protect the illusion of my perfect life for as long as I could.

Predictably, my parents had the opposite impulse.

"So! Where is our little Ronny?" they asked.

I smiled and motioned to the stroller parked right behind me in the crowd of arriving passengers. Tugging Ronny's hat down snug and deftly giving his chin a final swab, I wheeled him around to face them. I studied their faces as they leaned down and beheld him for the first time.

Ronny rested languidly in his stroller, passively absorbing the unusual sights and sounds of the airport. My parents noticed that Ronny was not normal, but they did not immediately press me with questions, perhaps because the airport was so busy. During the car ride home, the conversation focused on the girls, the scenery of Boston, Zvi's work, and how much they had missed us. I sensed that my parents were holding their questions about Ronny until a more appropriate time.

We arrived at the house, removed the baggage from the car, and helped my parents settle into their room. Aware of their jetlag, we fed them a light meal and sent them off to bed. As the door latched behind them, I breathed a sigh of relief. We had successfully avoided talking about Ronny's problems, at least for one day.

That night, I decided that in addition to being Ronny's defender and cheerleader, I would also be his interpreter. The next morning, from the moment my parents came downstairs for breakfast, I began to supervise their interactions with Ronny. Not once did I allow them to be alone with him, not because they were untrustworthy, but because I felt a compulsive need to shape their opinion of him (and me) through explanation, commentary, and diversion.

Deep down, I knew that I was fooling no one. I could spin the truth only so much, especially with people who had known and loved me for so long. Nevertheless, I plowed on, undeterred in my role as the cheery and impervious mother. Silently, I pled for everyone else to play along. And for the most part, they did.

I remember only two "slips" in the act. The first came from my mother. The exact goings-on that preceded that moment remain lost to me, but I was taken aback when I heard her suddenly let out a sob.

"Why you? You don't deserve this!" she cried.

She could no longer contain her lament. Stoicism was my father's strong suit, not hers. I stared at her blankly, unsure of what to say. I do not remember what my next line was, but like an actress well-versed in her craft, I never broke character. I did not want my own lament to attract pity, and I especially did not want to be pitied by the woman who had filled our home with melancholy. We breezed past the interruption and never brought it up again.

My father, on the other hand, never openly departed from the script. He never probed. But that look of *knowing* would occasionally appear in his eyes. A couple of days before my parents flew home, he and I were sitting together in the backyard, watching over Ronny as he sat contentedly hunched in his sandbox. I was chattering away like the birds, making breezy conversation, and feeling proud of Ronny for remaining propped up by himself. I felt relaxed in the presence of my Abba and untroubled by my usual worries. Then, I noticed that my father was gazing at Ronny. Something told me that he could see our situation clearly, maybe with even greater lucidity than I possessed. He must have felt my eyes on him because the moment lasted only a second or two before he looked up at me, gave me a gentle smile, and settled back in his seat to look up at the sky. That moment broke my heart.

A few days later, when the time came for my parents to leave, I felt a mix of sadness and relief. Their presence in our home had not been without sweetness, but navigating the family dynamics and straining to uphold the appearance of perfection—to keep everyone on script—had taxed my energy. I was ready to let down my guard. And yet, at the thought of their departure, I could feel myself suppressing despondency.

As I helped my parents load their luggage into the trunk of our car, it struck me that my parents were going home to Israel *and I was not.* I had listened all morning to them talking about upcoming projects, buying groceries, and visiting friends and neighbors in Ein Kerem. It stung to know that they would return to a normal life in the place I loved. For the first time, I looked a long-avoided truth dead in the eye.

I'm not going back to Israel.

Not today. Not in a year or two, when Ronny "got better." In fact, for as long as Ronny was alive, not ever. I might visit Israel, but it would not be *home* for a long time. Maybe ever again.

I again felt trapped within the walls, locked in a situation I had not chosen and could not control. The reward for all my heartache—moving home to Israel—was no more than a mirage. Ronny's walls would never fully come down, and because love bound me to him, I would never get my old life back. America would have to become home.

CHAPTER SEVENTEEN

YEARS IN FRAGMENTS

chro·nol·o·gy / krəˈnäləjē / noun: The arrangement of events or dates in the order of their occurrence.

Out of monuments, names, words, proverbs, traditions, private records and evidences, fragments of stories, passages of books, and the like, do we save and recover somewhat from the deluge of time.
– Francis Bacon[i]

Sometimes I would let clutter accumulate in my room like an invasive plant. When I could restrain myself no longer, I would set everything aright: smooth the creases on my bedspread, make tidy stacks of books and papers, arrange bunches of hand-picked flowers to beautify the bare walls of my high-windowed bedroom. Once finished, I would stand back to take it all in, to feel the pleasure of a world "put together."

Clocks cannot tell our time of day
For what event to pray,
Because we have not time, because
We have not time until
We know what time we fill . . .
– W.H. Auden[ii]

In 1941, Boris III, the tsar of Bulgaria, joined the Axis Pact. This, despite his previous claims that, "My ministers are pro-German, my wife is pro-Italian, my people are pro-Russian—I am the only neutral in the country." History has, at times, condemned him as a "puppet king" or "dictator," but the tsar has also been commended for having had both the integrity and the audacity to stand up to his Axis allies. Evidently sympathetic to the sentiments of his pro-Russian people, he refused Germany's requests to send troops to fight with them against Russia on the Eastern Front. Nor did he stop there. Later, Boris III defied Hitler's demands to deport Bulgaria's Jewish population to concentration camps in Poland (although, his critics point out, he failed to show the same boldness on behalf of the eleven thousand Jews who were deported from the Bulgarian territories in Macedonia and the Balkans). To mask his insolence, the tsar explained to the fuhrer that he was having roads and railroads constructed all around Bulgaria and he needed the Jews to serve as his labor force. He then placed Jewish men in forced labor camps where "men were treated well, furloughed on weekends, and released during the winters, conditions that did not escape the notice of the Nazis."[iii] What *did* escape the Nazis' notice was that the tsar's stalling and obfuscating *had made time* for grassroots rescue efforts to discreetly remove more than fifty thousand Bulgarian Jews from the fuhrer's reach.[iv]

In the Talmud it reads, "If you have guarded your mouth from evil speech, your days will be peaceful."[v] And the wisdom of Proverbs says, "Whoever pursues righteousness and love finds life, prosperity and honor."[vi] Gaining such wisdom takes time, and the wise person knows that these statements are only true *in principle* . . .

In mathematics, I was introduced to the order of operations. Always begin inside the parentheses. Then simplify all exponents. Next, multiply and divide, and finally, add and subtract. Understanding the order of operations meant that, no matter how long or convoluted an equation appeared, I could always follow the same methodology and arrive at the correct solution. Later, in science class, I found out that humans could learn about Earth's physical laws by applying experimental methods. Outcomes could be consistently predicted, tested, and confirmed. $E=mc^2$ never changes. Rays of light always bend in the presence of a strong gravitational field. If there is no interference, an object at rest stays at rest. In my experience, the certainty of physical laws does not seem to apply to the human condition. Someday I would like to know why not.

There is a Talmudic proverb that says, "Good deeds always cause more good deeds."[vii] If that were true, surely Boris III would have been rewarded for his heroism with life, prosperity, and honor. Instead, it is believed that he *paid* with his life. In August 1943, the tsar was summoned for a meeting with Hitler, who was infuriated by his lack of cooperation. Germany was losing the war and his Bulgarian "ally" seemed to have gone rogue. Although the meeting's occurrence was later denied, many claimed that the conference between the fuhrer and the tsar devolved into a tempestuous confrontation. Two weeks later, at age forty-nine, Boris III died suddenly, apparently of a heart attack. Many people suspected poison.

When Ronny was born, the neat, linear storyline of life shattered. The once rational and systematic world felt arbitrary and chaotic, fragmented. Nothing held together. Attempts to reconstruct my life only made the situation worse. The shards flew off in disparate directions, like debris in space. When there is no gravity, and there wasn't, an object in motion stays in motion. Yet, I told myself, *I can fix this.*

ex·po·nen·tial   / ekspə'nen(t)SH(ə)l / adjective:
(of an increase) becoming more and more rapid.

Trucks pulling into a cobbled schoolyard, coming to smuggle people out of their hometown to safety. Refugees in their own country. Exiles who had been been exiled again.

"Studying the Talmud is not about reading the text to extract the 'right' answers," said our teacher, who was a seven-fingered soldier and scholar. "It's about learning to ask questions and listening to opposing viewpoints until you are able to reconcile two seemingly incongruous things." Our debates and dialogues felt like mathematics with words, like balancing a chemical equation.

"The one who gets wisdom loves life; the one who cherishes understanding will soon prosper."[viii]

The sign on the door read, "Early Intervention Group—Families Welcome." Inside the brightly lit room, I sat uneasily in a wide circle of chairs. Ronny and I were regular attendees of this group, but whereas Ronny (an eight-year-old extrovert) sat guileless and giddy beside me, I felt vulnerable. Every week, I felt like a sober person who had accidentally stumbled into an Alcoholics Anonymous meeting. "Sorry," I always wanted to say, "There must be some mistake. I don't belong here." I *did* belong there. This group was designed to serve people like me, to create a support system for people like me, to show people like me that we were not alone. However, I had no desire to be lumped in with these people like me. They looked frazzled and unkempt. They wore baggy jeans and sweatshirts. I felt no solidarity with them; rather, I felt (guiltily) competitive. Where did Ronny and I "rank"? *At least we are not that dysfunctional. But look, that girl is higher functioning than Ronny.* At home, I felt both shame and longing for a normal life. Still, I wished I did not belong in that group of people like me.

Nostalgia, according to the Oxford English Dictionary, refers to a "sentimental imagining or evocation of a period of the past," or, for me, a longing for the orderly, formulaic ways of life before Ronny. The natural order of life is often heard in songs for children. My daughters, while playing with a friend in the front yard, chanted this song obsessively. ". . . First comes love, then comes marriage, then comes baby in a baby carriage!"

The spotlights obscure the large audience and TV cameras from my view. "I would like to go to college, get married, and have six children!" Laughter erupts.

Why, after two healthy pregnancies, had I given birth to a son with severe disabilities? Zvi saw no reason to ask such questions. "What's done is done," he would say. He was probably right, but that did not stop the questions from coming. Doctors never matched Ronny's case to another's. When pressed, they would shrug and say, "Probably a fluke mutation."

`flu·ke` / flo͞ok / noun: an unlikely chance occurrence, especially a surprising piece of luck.

You call *this* luck?

Her knees buckling mid-stride. Her shorn head slumping. The ghastly sound of the gunshot echoing off the cold, impervious brick buildings.

"Come! Come! Flee from the land of the north," declares the Lord, "for I have scattered you to the four winds of heaven," declares the Lord.[ix]

a·li·yah / aliyá / noun: an ascent; elevation; going up; the act of proceeding to the reading table in a synagogue; the immigration of Jews to Israel, either as individuals or in groups.[x]

While growing up, most of the adults I knew had "made aliyah." By choice or by force, they had followed the biblical command to "go up" to the land of Israel, which is not always topographically higher than the lands from which these people came. The highest peak inside Israel's borders is Mount Hermon—a mere 2,236 meters. Jerusalem, the holy city, is just 754 meters above sea level. Thus, the words "making aliyah" refer to the belief that Israel is the Holy Land, the Promised Land, the land that God set aside for his people.

The Talmud ingrained this belief into us from a young age. It quotes from Deuteronomy: "And you shall arise and go up to the place that the Lord, your God, shall choose" (Deuteronomy 17:8). "This," according to rabbinical analysis, "teaches that the Temple is higher than all Eretz Yisrael, which is why the verse speaks of ascending from the cities of Eretz Yisrael to the Temple. And it teaches that Eretz Yisrael is higher than all the lands."[xi] In typical Talmudic debates, a natural question arises. "But from where do we derive the claim that Eretz Yisrael is higher than all other lands?" the text asks. In answer, the Talmudic sages point to the words of Jeremiah. "As it is written: 'Therefore behold, the days are coming, says the Lord, when they shall no more say: As the Lord lives, Who brought up the children of Israel out of the land of Egypt, but: As the Lord lives, Who brought up and Who led the seed of the house of Israel out of the north country, and from all the countries where I had driven them' (Jeremiah 23:7–8). The phrase 'Who brought up' indicates that Eretz Yisrael is higher than all the other lands from where God will bring the Jewish people."[xii]

The religiously observant clung to these words, believing there was inherent righteousness in the act of moving *to* and subsequently living *in* the land of Israel. Even irreligious Israeli citizens agreed that "making aliyah" was not just desirable, but honorable. To immigrate to Israel was to move up in the world. To step onto Israeli soil was a near-transcendent experience. To live there was to be unspeakably blessed.

"Look homeward angel."
– John Milton, *Lycidas*

ye·ri·da / yeridá / noun: descent; going down; the emigration of Jews from Israel

Yerida was like a dirty word. Something mumbled or spat. Why would anyone leave Israel? Exile? Diaspora? Such an existence, whether chosen or imposed, imbued people with disgrace, just as aliyah imbued people with honor. *But it's not really a yerida*, I had told myself. *I'm not emigrating. I'm going on a one-year trip. An adventure.* Still, part of me felt like a deserter.

Yerida l'shem aliyah. This Jewish maxim elevates yerida by declaring that descent is a necessary precursor to ascent. You can only go high if you have first gone low. Look at Israel's biblical forefathers. Did God not promise Abraham, the childless Jewish patriarch, that he would make his descendants into a great nation and give to them the land of Canaan? The fulfillment of this promise did not come in the manner they expected. They entered Canaan, but a famine soon forced Abraham and Sarah to "go down" (yerida) to Egypt.[xiii] Did this elderly, barren couple—pressed to choose between survival and staying in the land they had been promised—feel like deserters? Did they feel deserted? . . . God had not abandoned them. Abraham and Sarah gave birth to a son, Isaac, and eventually returned to the Promised Land to live out the rest of their days. Abraham and Sarah went high because they first were brought low.

My parents' generation witnessed evil firsthand. They had learned—either from experience or by observation—that life does not always play fair. People living quiet, peaceful lives one day could be carted off like cattle the next. A human being could go from "fit for labor" to "target practice" in less time than it had taken to tattoo a serial number on a forearm. Opposing injustice could lead to assassination. Nevertheless, senseless evil leaves survivors with a choice: to despair or to rebuild. Those who chose the latter learned to cherish life's beauty while shouldering its hardships.

As children, we sang songs by people like Arik Einstein and Yehonatan Geffen. The lyrics promised that, together, Israelis could overcome adversity and change the world. We could build and be rebuilt. I sometimes hummed the songs, wondering how their words might apply to me as I stumbled through mundane days in a foreign city so far from home.

Many years after Abraham and Sarah's yerida and aliyah, the land of Canaan faced another famine. This time, it was their grandson, Jacob, and his twelve sons who were forced to either "go down" to Egypt or die. Jacob, familiar with God's covenant with Abraham, must have wondered if leaving Canaan was the right thing to do. God comforted him, saying, "Do not be afraid to go down to Egypt, for I will make you into a great nation there. I will go down with you to Egypt, and I will surely bring you back, and [your son] Joseph's own hand will close your eyes."[xiv] The promise of return held true, but not within Jacob's lifetime. His body was only brought back to Canaan *to be buried*. His descendants spent *four hundred years* in Egypt as slaves before re-entering the Promised Land. Jacob certainly did not expect to make this kind of aliyah, nor did he imagine it would take so long.

Many Hebrew proverbs convey a world governed by causality. They are formulaic. Do A and B and you will get C. Cultivate wisdom and kindness and you'll spend your life in the Promised Land, or choose the way of the sluggard and your life will be littered with obstacles. Cause and effect. Take your pick. These sayings are part of the wisdom literature for a reason, so we pass them from generation to generation. However, sometimes choosing the right, moral, and loving path requires sacrifice. What happens when choosing love leads you down (yerida), far away from the Promised Land?

As Ronny grew older and as my daughters became young women, I decided to keep doing the right thing, to love the people in my life and to believe that life, despite its sorrows, is indeed beautiful. Zvi and I decided to have more children. Two more wonderful sons joined our family. While living and working in the US, we embarked on a different type of aliyah, the upward trajectory of love within a family. By now I knew that choosing this path of goodness would not necessarily, like math, lead to an idyllic life.

I think there is another, more accurate formula. It was expressed well by poet T.S. Eliot.

> *Between the idea*
> *And the reality*
> *Between the motion*
> *And the act*
> *Falls the shadow.*[xv]

CHAPTER EIGHTEEN

THE INTRUDER

Poets and philosophers have been known to make broad, dramatic statements about suffering. Most are vague and unhelpful. Take the words of Arisotle, for example: "To perceive is to suffer." Or Walt Whitman's succinct summary: "I was a man. I suffered. I was there." True, perhaps, but not helpful.

We all hope to avoid suffering. We shut our doors and bar our windows in hopes of keeping it out. Despite our best efforts, hardships just waltz past our insular defenses and intrude our bodies, our apartments, our loved ones.

That is what suffering does: it intrudes. Intrusion is its specialty. Its mission is to shatter our naïveté and confront us with our vulnerability.

For me, this happened when Ronny was born. At the time, it seemed unfair that something completely outside of my control—"a fluke mutation"—could have such devastating and long-lasting effects on my son, our family, and the life I had worked so hard to build. At first, I looked for an escape. I wanted to rewind the clock, put Ronny up for adoption, "fix" him—*anything* to get back to an easier life that was under my control.

A mark of true suffering (versus mere discomfort) is that there is no way out. I could not turn back time. My heart and mind would have been tormented by guilt if I had given Ronny up for adoption. It was not within my power to "fix" him. I had no choice but to soldier on. Day by day, I had to choose to shoulder the weight and keep marching, just as I had done during the IDF Beret March. With Ronny, the path often seemed dark and impossibly steep, but I gradually found that I had greater capacity for suffering than I had imagined. As time passed—despite the fragmentation of my original plan for life—my view of the "burden" began to shift. I found new ways to carry the weight.

For one, I began to see that Ronny was a gift to our family. Physically, he had endured greater suffering than any of us, and yet he possessed an unconditional love for everyone who met him. Just like each of our kids, he offered something to our family that was unique. Without him, we would have been incomplete.

Twenty years had passed since Ronny's traumatic birth. In addition to the typical duties of being a wife, a mom, and (eventually) a business partner to Zvi, I was also Ronny's primary caretaker and advocate. I was responsible for meeting his day-to-day needs, which included setting up appointments, surgeries, therapies, programs, or services. I pushed him to achieve things the doctors had never imagined possible, such as learning to walk. Unable to speak, he needed me to be his voice. As a result, Ronny made remarkable progress and grew to adulthood.

Despite his victories, Ronny's extensive medical issues prevented him from attaining even basic independence. He remained like a small child—never able to speak, go to high school, or live on his own. His needs were always changing and evolving. Thus, my "backpack" never became light.

Moments of joy and gratitude were mercifully embedded within the exhaustion and distress. Ronny, as a perpetual child, approached life with an infectious guilelessness, wonder, and delight. He loved gourmet food, often surprising us with his hearty appetite. He also loved movies and took great satisfaction in scanning the shelves of outward-facing DVD cases that lined the perimeter of his room. More than food or movies, he loved music. He owned an impressive collection of CDs that represented his appreciation for many genres and artists. He could contentedly listen for hours on end, bobbing his head to the music and smiling at us each time a favorite song came on. *Live* music was even better. It mesmerized him, so we often took him to concerts and watched his face light up with joy. Music was such a passion for him that, if not for his disabilities, Ronny might have become a musician. Perhaps he got this trait from my father, who was a gifted singer and music lover.

Ronny's greatest love was people. Like my father, he had a magnetism that drew people to him wherever we went. From nurses to grocery store clerks to his siblings' classmates and friends, everyone loved him. And he loved them back. We, the members of his family, were lucky enough to receive the greatest outpouring of that love. Ronny's face lit up whenever one of his siblings walked into the room. I often caught him staring adoringly at them for no apparent reason.

Ronny's love was unique. Here was a person who had no ulterior motives, expectations, or judgments. He was never stressed or in a hurry, nor did he become cross or exasperated. You could sit in silence with him for hours and never feel pressure to say something, or you could speak your mind unfiltered and never worry that he would be annoyed. I knew Ronny loved me with no strings attached. When the whole family was gathered around the dinner table, eating, talking, and laughing, Ronny would catch my eye and make the sign for *happy*, which was one of the few words he knew in sign language. Those moments of connection between the two of us, when I knew that Ronny was not just okay but thriving, made all the moments of suffering and sacrifice seem worthwhile.

Those twenty years felt like one long lesson in cultivating resilience. Daily, I had a choice: succumb to bitterness, self-pity, and fatalism, or practice joy, gratitude, and optimism. Some days I chose well and on others I fell short, but as time went on it got easier to carry the burdens. I was reaching a point in the march where the horizon was beginning to reveal the faintest hues of light.

Like I said, suffering is an expert intruder.

When Ronny was twenty-one, Zvi was diagnosed with cancer. The doctors told us that he had non-Hodgkin's lymphoma, a cancer that attacks the lymphatic system. He would need to begin treatments immediately. Just as I was feeling adjusted to life, the news felt like the weight of my pack and the length of my trek had doubled. Our lives were about to get much harder.

I had naively believed that suffering would only strike once. Like the Exodus story, when the Passover lamb's blood was painted over doorframes to protect the Israelites, I had believed that our situation with Ronny would mark us as "off limits" against further devastation. Zvi's cancer taught me that suffering does not respect limits.

As his treatments began, I found that my resilience "muscle" was already strong. I knew how to respond. This would be another round of true suffering, meaning that there was no escape, but being Ronny's mother had taught me that I did not have to let suffering crush me. I could find a way to shoulder more weight.

Zvi, as usual, took the blow with resolute stoicism. When I asked how we should break the news to our kids and his parents, he calmly forbade me from telling anyone. "Why should we ask them to carry such a burden?" he asked. "I might overcome it." The thought of keeping such a secret appalled me at first, but as I listened to his reasoning, I began to see Zvi's desire to protect those he loved. He was convinced that the diagnosis would be more traumatic for our kids than for him. We knew that the type of lymphoma he had was considered to be one of the "easier" cancers to treat, so he was hopeful that he could beat it before the family ever had to find out. Nevertheless he agreed to tell them—and prepare them mentally and emotionally—if the situation deteriorated.

I decided to help Zvi keep the diagnosis private for as long as possible. Keeping the secret meant that I had to assume an additional burden in relation to our children. At the time, our three sons lived at home and our two daughters, then in their twenties, lived on their own. For three years, Zvi and I had to conceal paperwork, medicine bottles, phone calls, and conversations about his health from the kids. In the meantime, Zvi and I did our best to maintain normalcy. While I was taking care of our sons, Zvi ran the textile manufacturing company that he had founded in 1991.

I was responsible for covertly coordinating and taking Zvi to his twice-weekly cancer treatments. On those mornings, we would drop the three boys off at their respective schools and drive to Boston's North End for two fortifying cups of cappuccino before heading to the hospital for Zvi's chemotherapy. Afterward, Zvi would go to the office—feeling bedraggled. This enabled him to get through the worst side effects without the kids knowing. It was a surreal and intense time.

After three years it became clear that Zvi's cancer treatments were not working. The cancer had become more aggressive. The doctors told us that the next step would be a bone marrow transplant, a risky procedure. It did not take a doctor to see that Zvi's situation was looking grimmer each day. With increasing frequency, Zvi was forced to stay home from work, silently enduring his pain in the privacy of our bedroom. The kids—even Ronny—were growing suspicious. The time had come to tell them the truth.

They were crushed. Some yelled and some got quiet. All of them (except Ronny) felt betrayed. I understood how they felt, but I could not bring myself to fault Zvi for wanting to hope, for those three years, that he would pull through. I also could not fault Zvi or myself for wanting to protect our kids. All parents hope to minimize the suffering of their children. In the case of ours, the need to care for Ronny made their lives harder than most. Seeing their reactions that day, I began to wonder whether the effort to shield them from Zvi's illness had debilitated their resilience. Had we sufficiently equipped them to endure whatever might lie ahead, or had we made them weaker? It was a scary question, but I had to believe that they were more resilient than they realized. They, too, would have to decide to shoulder the weight of the packs they had been handed and soldier on.

☙❧

While we waited to find out whether Zvi qualified for a bone marrow transplant, we continued to hold our weekly Shabbat dinner. A central practice of Judaism, these meals take place every Friday evening at sundown. They typically signify the commencement of the Sabbath, the Jewish day of rest. Zvi and I had grown up enjoying the practice, so for decades we maintained the tradition in our Boston home. These dinners provided a chance for the family to come together, slow down, remember our Israeli roots, and delight in the food. They infused our lives with the peace, or *shalom*, that comes from *being* instead of *doing*.

Zvi and I also felt an increasing need to take a family vacation in Israel while he was still feeling well enough, and while his treatment plan was in limbo. The break from routine, a chance to take our minds off Zvi's cancer for a couple weeks, and a little sunshine would be therapeutic for us. We made all the plans, informed family and friends, and bought the plane tickets.

On the afternoon before our departure, while I was wrapping up our last-minute Shabbat dinner preparations, the phone rang. On the line was a person who over many years had become extremely dear to my heart and for whom I felt a life-long responsibility. (I have chosen to keep her anonymous in this book for the sake of her privacy.) She said, in a troubled voice, that she had just been diagnosed with a life-threatening illness.

They say that the eye of a hurricane is completely calm. For a moment, I felt like I was in the eye. Everything slowed down and sound faded.

Please let me disappear, I thought. *Not her, too. I can't do this anymore.*

Then, as if the eye of the storm had swept over me, I was back in the thundering, swirling storm. I immediately knew that she would need me to help her through the coming months of medical care. She needed me to be strong, yet everything in me wanted to collapse to the ground and cry. Somehow, I took another step in the march. I listened, reassured her, and pointed to reasons for hope. My words did not assuage our fears.

After I hung up, I dropped to the floor weeping. *This can't be happening,* I thought.

Shalom, that night at least, had come to naught. Through the panic, I began to strategize the required immediate steps. I knew that I would not be able to travel to Israel, so I set about canceling flights. I knew there would be *more* hospital visits, *more* doctors, *more* treatment plans, *more* difficult decisions, *more* suffering. I wept some more.

Just then, one of my sons walked in. He could tell something was seriously wrong. I tried to hide my tears, but I had been caught off guard and could not compose myself fast enough. Through my tears, I told him the news. I admitted to him that, after the last three grueling years with Zvi, I was afraid.

He stood just inside the door, stoically, like his father. I could not discern what he was thinking. Then he walked over, gently pulled me to my feet, and embraced me. It felt like I was holding a tree in the hurricane.

"It's going to be okay," he assured me. "We'll get through this."

In that moment, I saw my son's resilience and courage. After years of being strong for my kids, but always worrying that I was overprotecting them, it was emboldening to see my son lending his strength *to me.* He lifted me out of the dust and reminded me that I was not alone.

The subsequent months centered on caring for two seriously ill, beloved people. It seemed like trench warfare, with life and death at stake. This is not a book about IVs and pills and . . . I see no need to elaborate on the emotional toll or the physical workload, but it was exhausting. There was no escape. So, as always, I had to *choose*. Either do the right thing in the midst of suffering—love people—or quit. Every time I thought I had reached the ceiling of what I could endure, I somehow found the strength.

Mercifully, the woman whom I love so dearly overcame her illness. Zvi, however, was taken from us in 2005. To the end, he remained the same strong, reliable, compelling man that I had met as a teenager. As I watched him slip away, I often reflected on those early days of our relationship. My nineteen-year-old self could never have anticipated how desperately I would need a partner like him: loyal, predictable, and indomitable in the face of every storm. How grateful I am that I sidelined all the suave-but-fickle boys who had courted me with starry eyes and love poems. Zvi was affectionate and often romantic, but he mostly displayed his love by remaining at my side through every trial. In the end, we had built a life and family that we could be proud of. Aliyah.

CHAPTER NINETEEN

THE PAINTING

Throughout Ronny's life, I had tried to bring down his walls, to expand his limits. As he grew into adulthood, I began to discern which walls were immovable. Consequently, I spent less energy trying to expand Ronny's boundaries and more time enhancing his quality of life. I showered him with affection, enrolled him in excellent programs and services, and lobbied for everything possible that might help him. Ronny's calendar was always full of fun outings and activities.

On a couple of occasions, I set Ronny up in living situations where he could experience a semblance of independence, such as an apartment with a roommate (who I paid to be his caretaker). Those attempts did not succeed for long and Ronny always landed back home. This worked for a time, but after Zvi had passed away and the other kids had all moved out, I realized that caring for Ronny alone was neither sustainable for me nor fair to him. I still worked full-time running Zvi's business and our home. It had once bustled with people and activity, but now it felt empty. Ronny needed something better.

After a couple of years, I made the painful decision to sell the house and move Ronny into a group home. Handing his day-to-day care off to someone else—after more than thirty years of being his primary caretaker—was not easy. But I felt sure that this option was the best way to provide Ronny with the highest quality of life. After careful research, I found a group home that would keep Ronny safe and fill his days with positive relationships and activities. He also continued to attend the same daily rehabilitation program that had been part of his life for years. His siblings, friends, physical trainer, and I visited him regularly in the group home. We often took Ronny on outings—horseback rides, library programs, movies, concerts, restaurants—anything that would put a smile on his face. He *never* felt "shuffled off" or forgotten. Due to my frequent presence, the group home's staff knew that I was keeping tabs on Ronny's care. As his needs and mine changed, we found new ways to shoulder the backpack. My father's words, "If I am only for myself, what am I?", carried me through many difficult days. Love infused the hardships with meaning and joy. He knew I loved him. He loved me back.

Ronny *never* had an easy day.
He triumphed over the opinions and predictions of many doctors.
He knocked down many walls, but some would not fall.
His body began to lose more fights.
I could see that mother and son would soon have to say goodbye.
I spent even more time with him, filling him with love.
Doctors once said he would not survive infancy.
Ronny lived to be thirty-nine.
His valiant march was over.

It was time to set down my backpack. After Ronny died, I felt like a soldier extracted from the trenches. For decades, life had felt like a long firefight: no time to philosophize, everything mission critical, shore up the family's weakest links, eliminate looming threats, prepare for the next barrage. Now, with Zvi and Ronny gone and the rest of the kids living on their own, the intensity turned to calm. I had time to think about the meaning of the past and to consider my next steps.

As a young girl, I had thought of life as a blank canvas and of myself as its artist. I had a picture in mind of what I wanted to create, and I felt confident that with hard work and proper techniques I could make the painting match what I had envisioned. Over the years, I set to work. I introduced color here and detail there, adding each new element deliberately so as to not make mistakes. I wanted to paint a picture that would make my parents proud, one that would inspire others with its perfection and beauty. For twenty-seven years, the painting came together as I had imagined. I had health, beauty, loving parents, a good education, a devoted husband, beautiful children, and a promising career trajectory. I just needed to add a few more kids and a return to Israel before my picture would be (in my mind) complete.

When I found out that my newborn son was severely disabled, the news felt like watching a vandal barge into my studio and splatter red paint across my canvas. The vandal was a fluke genetic mutation, yet it seemed to have ruined my painting. Ronny's long-term disabilities made it seem like nothing else in the painting could even be noticed, let alone appreciated. I became so fixated on Ronny that I failed to pay attention to the rest of the painting. The splotch of paint could not be concealed. There was no way to artfully cover over it. My painting was irrevocably changed.

Why me? I had asked.

Crushing disappointments are common in life. Eventually, we all see that we do not have full control over our destinies. We can keep every rule, follow all the best formulas, exercise self-discipline, and still end up with the "intruder" in our homes. There is simply no way to protect the canvas from the vandal.

But we do have a choice. We *always* have a choice. Will we give in to self-pity and let suffering become the lens through which we see the world? Will we quit and walk away into a life of selfish pursuits? Or will we face the hardship and resolve to make something beautiful?

It might be tempting to think that some people are born with resilience and others are not, but I am living proof that resilience is something we choose to develop. Any ordinary person can do it. One need not be a superhero. Mental and emotional strength improve in the same way that physical strength does. Stress (in the form of exercise) will make our bodies stronger and the avoidance of stress leads to physical weakness. Likewise, emotional resilience is like a muscle. We can become stronger because of stress and hardship. We can choose to train ourselves to be more resilient.

My resilience training happened inadvertently. As a girl, I was exposed to people who had gone through great suffering. They taught me that hardship is neither uncommon nor damning, so "Why *not* me?" As a young woman in the IDF, I learned that limits are often imagined barriers, not real ones. I learned not to listen when my mind and emotions tried to convince me to quit. The more I pushed beyond my perceived limits, the greater my threshold for physical stress became. Later in life, these lessons helped me strengthen my mind and emotions.

Unfortunately, the path of perseverance is the harder choice. It is far easier to choose self-pity and despair. The word *despair* means "without hope." When a person is going through a time of suffering, it is hard to see hope—at first. Thus, the path of despair seems natural, almost logical. However, it is a lie that never leads to anything good or beautiful.

Hope takes courage. Zvi had that courage. When I told him about Ronny, he looked adversity in the eye and said, "I don't know about you, but I think life is beautiful." Then he went out and made it so. Ronny courageously chose hope, too. Despite his limitations, he loved the people in his life and displayed his sign for *happy*. All my other children also chose hope. They have courageously persevered to build their own lives while standing firmly together through our family's hardships. I can see now that we transformed a vandalized painting into a beautiful work of art.

Artists often speak about coming to a crossroads when their vision for a painting or sculpture does not materialize. Their first option is to fixate on the problem, obsessing over how miserably it has fallen short of what they had originally envisioned. Sometimes they choose to abandon the project.

The seasoned artist will consider a second option: stop fixating on the problem, step back, and reflect on the work as a whole. Seeing the entire picture, these artists often find that the problem is not as ruinous as it first seemed. Rather, they see that the flaw is complemented by the surrounding beauty. They see a way—with creativity—for the work to be redeemed.

Ronny was a gift. He gave me a new color with which to paint. Each family member added a unique splash of color to the canvas. Now, when I step back and look at the entire work, I can see how all the hardships became integral to the art.

My life did not play out according to plan. Neither will yours. May we all respond with courage, reshoulder our packs, set our eyes on the horizon, and soldier on.

ENDNOTES

ⁱ   Cited in George Seldes, *The Great Thoughts,* New York: Random House, 1985, p. 26.

ⁱⁱ   W.H. Auden, "No Time," in *Collected Shorter Poems, 1927-1957,* New York: Vintage, 1975.

ⁱⁱⁱ   https://old.post-gazette.com/magazine/20000321bulgaria1.asp

^{iv}   http://content.time.com/time/subscriber/article/0,33009,802945,00.html; https://www.newworldencyclopedia.org/entry/Boris_III_of_Bulgaria; https://www.britannica.com/biography/Boris-III; https://www.newworldencyclopedia.org/entry/Boris_III_of_Bulgaria; https://www.latimes.com/archives/la-xpm-1994-05-23-mn-61215-story.html.

^v   Derech Eretz Zuta 9

^{vi}   Proverbs 21:21

^{vii}   Talmud, Tractate Avot 4:2

^{viii}   Proverbs 19:8

^{ix}   Zechariah 2:6

^x   https://www.dictionary.com/browse/aliyah

^{xi}   Talmud (Kiddushin 69a) https://www.sefaria.org/Kiddushin.69a.15?ven=William_Davidson_Edition_-_English&vhe=William_Davidson_Edition_-_Vocalized_Aramaic&lang=bi

^{xii}   Talmud (Kiddushin 69b) https://www.sefaria.org/Kiddushin.69b.1?ven=William_Davidson_Edition_-_English&vhe=William_Davidson_Edition_-_Vocalized_Aramaic&lang=bi&with=all&lang2=en

^{xiii}   Genesis 12:10

^{xiv}   Genesis 46:3-4

^{xv}   T.S. Eliot, "The Hollow Men," in *The American Tradition in Literature, Volume II,* New York: Random House, 1985, p. 1088.

ACKNOWLEDGEMENTS

Writing *Soldier On* would not have been possible alone. First and foremost, I want to thank my children and grandchildren for all the ways they have encouraged and inspired me to tell my story. I would also like to thank my sister for her love and loyalty throughout the years. Special gratitude goes to my partner, who has believed in me and walked beside me through every step of this journey. And of course, I could never forget the many dear friends who provided me with their invaluable companionship and cheered me on.

This book would not exist without the special and talented writer (and de facto therapist) Sophie Paulson, nor would it have been possible without the tireless effort of my publisher and editor Glenn McMahan. Many thanks to you both.

Lastly, I want to acknowledge the community of people with disabilities throughout the world who struggle daily, and who—due to no fault of their own—must cope with life-altering impediments. You make this world a better place.

To everyone mentioned above and all my loved ones who have gone before, thank you for adding so much color to my world.

ABOUT THE AUTHOR

Bracha Horovitz is a first-generation Israeli, a mother, entrepreneur, and businesswoman. Having served in the Israel Defense Forces and then becoming a runner-up in the Miss Israel beauty pageant, she went on to earn a degree in textile engineering. She has lived and worked in the United States while raising her children, including her son Ronny, who was born with severe disabilities. Bracha continues to advocate for parents with disabled children and the organizations who help them.